Fishing Boats of Campbeltown Shipyard

Fishing Boats of Campbeltown Shipyard

Sam Henderson & Peter Drummond

Frontispiece: One of the Campbeltown Shipyard's renowned 80ft seiners, *Fear Not* (INS197). (Peter Drummond)

First published 2009

The History Press
The Mill, Brimscombe Port
Stroud, Gloucestershire, GL5 2QG
www.thehistorypress.co.uk

© Sam Henderson and Peter Drummond, 2009

The right of Sam Henderson and Peter Drummond to be identified as the Authors of this work has been asserted in accordance with the Copyrights, Designs and Patents Act 1988.

All rights reserved. No part of this book may be reprinted or reproduced or utilised in any form or by any electronic, mechanical or other means, now known or hereafter invented, including photocopying and recording, or in any information storage or retrieval system, without the permission in writing from the Publishers.
British Library Cataloguing in Publication Data.
A catalogue record for this book is available from the British Library.

ISBN 978 0 7524 4765 0

Typesetting and origination by The History Press
Printed in Great Britain

Contents

Acknowledgements 6

Introduction 7

A-Z of Fishing Boats of Campbeltown Shipyard 23

Appendix I: Photo Miscellany 111

Appendix II: List of Vessels Built by Campbeltown Shipyard 124

Acknowledgements

We are indebted to a number or people for their assistance in the preparation of this book. Without the skill and generosity of photographic contributors David Linkie, Ian Leask, Peter Brady, John M. Addison, Tryggvi Sigurõsson, Michael Craine, George Young and Lenny McLaughlin this book would contain far fewer pictures and be much the poorer for it. We also acknowledge the help given by William and Dianne Strachan of Studio Nova in Peterhead.

When gathering information for this book we received a great deal of assistance from Jim Tarvit and the staff of the Scottish Fisheries Museum, Anstruther, and from Sue Fortune and the staff of Campbeltown Library. We must give Lenny McLaughlin a special mention for finding some very useful information in Ireland and we also acknowledge with thanks the assistance of Les Howarth, Norrie Bremner, Douglas McNaught, Lachie Paterson, Margaret Downey, Andrew Murdoch, Neil Wilson, Agnar Erlingsson, Bjorn Kristensen, Brendan Leonard and Brian McGuinness.

Introduction

When co-author Sam Henderson visited Campbeltown in April 2001, the empty buildings which once comprised Campbeltown Shipyard betrayed no trace of the hive of activity which once existed there and produced some of the most successful fishing vessels ever built in Scotland. True, the yard also built vessels other than fishing boats. Its production included a survey vessel; two ferries; two workboats; a brace of wellboats and a floating restaurant. It also built feed barges and fabricated fish cages for the fish-farming industry. But it is for the fishing boats that it will be remembered.

Shipbuilding in Campbeltown did not begin with Campbeltown Shipyard. In fact, the origins of boat building in the town are lost in the mists of time, possibly dating back as far as the creation of the town as a Royal Burgh in 1700. A shipbuilding and ship-repairing facility was situated at the head of the Old Quay during part of the eighteenth and nineteenth centuries. This yard built the 48-ton coastal brigantine, *Campbeltown*, plainly named after her birthplace, for owner W. Watson in 1793, but much of its production appears to have been coastal sloops. Examples include the 28-ton *Endeavour*, built for Andrew Ralston in 1800 and commanded by D. Campbell; the 60-ton *Harmony* built for R. & G. Colvill in 1817 and commanded by A. Colvill; and the 33-ton *Mayflower* built for Peter Stewart in 1818 and commanded by D. Cameron. This yard ceased operations in the 1830s.

In 1877, Archibald McEachan, a native of Campbeltown who had amassed a fortune as an African merchant, established a new yard at Trench Point. This yard was known as the Campbeltown Shipbuilding Co. It launched its first vessel, the 84ft schooner *May*, in 1878 and went on to build 116 ships, including the 4,363-ton SS *Roquelle*, the largest vessel ever built at Trench Point. The yard failed to survive the depression of the 1920s and delivered its last vessel, the SS *Akenside*, in 1922.

More than forty years were to pass before shipbuilding was revived at Trench Point. The resurgence of the trade was a consequence of the growing fortunes of the Scottish inshore fishing industry in the mid-1960s and the increasing abandonment of herring fishing in favour of white fish and shellfish catching.

In the mid-1960s, a sizeable part of the Scottish inshore fleet consisted of vessels designed and built for ring-net fishing and many of these had been delivered in the late 1940s. From around the mid-1950s, the ringers increasingly became multi-purpose vessels, spending their time between herring seasons seine netting for white fish or catching shellfish. In the

1960s, growing numbers of these boats began to abandon the ring net altogether and to devote themselves full time to what had begun as alternative fisheries.

In the 1960s, crews who persevered at the ring net began to face increasing competition from pair trawlers and latterly purse seiners in all of the traditional herring fisheries, but the move away from ring netting was well underway before the Scottish pair trawl and purse seine fleets developed the power they would wield in the early 1970s. Many of the ringers spent a great deal of time away from their home grounds, with the crews commonly being away for three to six weeks at a stretch. This became increasingly unacceptable to the crews, and the discovery of rich beds of shellfish off south-west Scotland and off the coast of Argyll meant that the substantial fleets of ringers based in Ayrshire and Kintyre could remain in their home waters, trawling for prawns or trawling or dredging for scallops instead of following the herring. Also, a vessel which would normally carry a six-man crew for the ring net could readily work with four men aboard when trawling.

There is nothing like successful fishing to encourage fishermen to build new boats and many vessels in the inshore fleet were becoming due for replacement as the 1960s wore on. Established Scottish boatbuilders continued to construct what were essentially traditional vessels, including ringers, though the new boats tended to be larger and more powerful than their predecessors. Some of the most enterprising fishermen began to look at the possibility of building boats which would not be a development of traditional vessels, but instead a radical departure therefrom. In particular, some skippers began to consider the construction of small boats built of steel instead of wood.

In terms of hull strength, steel has a considerable advantage over wood as a boat-building material. This is especially significant in the context of scallop dredging. The metal dredges cause heavy wear on a boat's sides and a wooden vessel cannot use them at all unless her hull is heavily protected with either wood reinforcing or steel sheathing. However well protected a wooden boat may be, a steel boat is better able to stand up to the rigours of dredging. Steel also has advantages over wood in terms of reduced overall maintenance, price and increased internal space within the boat.

It follows that steel is particularly suited to trawler construction. Whether or not a trawler engages in dredging, her hull is always subject to more wear and tear than that sustained in the gentler activities of ringing or seining, and trawling was becoming the primary objective of many of the inshore fleet, especially those well placed to exploit shellfish grounds. The crew of a trawler was spared the drudgery of carrying coils of seine net rope around the deck for much of the day, an activity which was inflicted on seiner crews before the advent of rope storage bins and reels. A trawler also retained the option of taking part in the herring fisheries. If the boat had a decent-sized engine, she could go to the herring pair trawl. At a pinch, she could even take part in ring netting as partner to a more traditional vessel. She would not be ideal for the ring net but she could do it.

It became increasingly likely that a completely new design of vessel would emerge and this happened in 1966 when Herd & Mackenzie of Buckie delivered the 50ft *Golden Strand* (BF403). *Golden Strand* was a steel stern trawler with her wheelhouse forward instead of in its usual location aft, and had a transom stern in place of the more normal rounded cruiser stern. Most importantly, she was a success. She was well able to cope with bad weather and was also a very effective catcher. In short, the new design worked.

Another yard, which entered the market for small steel vessels at an early stage, was Thames Launch Works Ltd of Eel Pie Island, Twickenham. This yard delivered the 40ft *Gleaner* (CN284) to Campbeltown skipper Cecil Finn in 1967 and the 47ft *Emma Will* (TH8) to English owners in 1968. *Gleaner* was probably the more significant vessel of the two, since she gave the yard an entry into the substantial Scottish market and, most significantly, she gave the yard a successful start. *Gleaner* was a steel-hulled, transom-sterned boat with her wheelhouse in its traditional position aft. She was fitted with a Kort nozzle around her propeller which proved highly satisfactory in practice. With the benefit of this device, *Gleaner*'s 110hp Gardner engine gave her a bollard pull of 39cwt compared to 29cwt for a more conventional vessel.

In 1968, Thames Launch Works Ltd set out to further establish its position in Scotland. The company set up a joint venture company originally called Thames Campbeltown Shipyard Ltd along with Ferguson Brothers (Port Glasgow) Ltd, a subsidiary of the Scott-Lithgow Group. The new company was promoted to construct a new yard at Trench Point, Campbeltown, on the site of Archibald McEachan's yard with financial assistance from the Highlands and Islands Development Board which contributed in excess of £100,000 to the project. Work on site commenced at the beginning of June that year and the completed yard, with a 160ft slipway capable of carrying a vessel of 300 tons displacement and 120ft in length, opened in December. In recognition of the historical significance of the site, a bell which once summoned workers to the old yard, was put on show in a glass case at the new shipyard.

Girl Seona (TT37), a 40ft sister to *Gleaner*, was ordered just too early to become the first vessel built by the yard. *Girl Seona* was built at Eel Pie Island, though she was brought north to Campbeltown to run her trials in Campbeltown Loch in 1969. The first boat to use the new yard was the local vessel *Albion* (CN45) which was slipped for overhaul in April 1969. Campbeltown Shipyard received its first order for a new fishing vessel in the same month when Skipper David Tod of Anstruther signed up for a 50ft (14.95m) steel stern trawler. Skipper Tod was so keen to have the first vessel built by the yard that he actually worked there as a marine engineer between August 1969 and April 1970, but local skipper James Macdonald's stern trawler *Crimson Arrow* (CN30) beat him to it, being launched into a wintry Campbeltown Loch on Wednesday, 18 February 1970. David Tod's *St Adrian* (KY245) followed Crimson Arrow down the slipway at the beginning of May.

The first launch – *Crimson Arrow* (CN30) slides down the slipway into Campbeltown Loch. (Courtesy Angus Martin)

Crimson Arrow and *St Adrian* were similar vessels but *St Adrian* was the more sophisticated of the two. *Crimson Arrow* was fitted with a conventional belt-driven trawl winch manufactured by D.F. Sutherland & Sons. *St Adrian* was fitted with a hydraulically driven combined winch and net drum manufactured by Smith Bros of Anstruther. She was in fact the first British trawler of any size to be designed around the use of a net drum. The unit fitted to *St Adrian* differed from most net drums by being constructed in two halves that could be separately driven. This was especially useful in squaring up the net if it came aboard unevenly and the use of the net drum allowed the trawl to be shot and hauled by two men, with the skipper working the winch controls.

The yard's third delivery was a 36ft survey vessel for the Manchester Ship Canal Co., but the Campbeltown small trawler design caught on among fishermen and the yard delivered the stern trawlers *Aquarian* (CN42), *Strathyre II* (LH200), *Jacquelynn Stuart* (LH159) and *Terra Nova* (A219) as well as the aft-wheelhouse *Steadfast* (LH90) by early 1972. *Jacquelynn Stuart* and *Terra Nova* began as speculative building projects, both of which found owners prior to completion.

In 1971, the yard also delivered an interesting variation of its stern trawler design that also began as a speculative project. The vessel concerned was the *Halcyon*, a 50ft fisheries research boat built for the Overseas Development Administration for use in Lake Rudolf in Kenya. Her extended wheelhouse included an electronics room for use by scientists. She had accommodation for eight men instead of the usual four and was fitted with a hydraulic trawl winch, line hauler and plankton sampler. She also had a hydraulic power block mounted on her aft gantry.

After running sea trials, *Halcyon* sailed to Glasgow where her wheelhouse and superstructure were removed, and the disassembled boat was loaded aboard the freighter *Clan McNab* for shipment to Mombassa. From Mombassa, *Halcyon* undertook an 800-mile overland journey to Lake Rudolph at a maximum speed of 10mph. The journey was not without incident as, seventy-five miles short of *Halcyon*'s destinationin deep in desert country, a heavy rainstorm led to the low loader becoming bogged down. Heavy recovery machinery had to be brought in to allow the vehicle to continue its journey to the lake where *Halcyon* was reassembled and fitted out under the supervision of the Campbeltown yard's foreman, John Carmichael, who had travelled out to Africa with the boat.

The 50-footers, designed by Leslie Howarth of Campbeltown Shipyard, were a considerable success for the yard. They had plenty of towing power, were economical on fuel and had excellent sea-keeping qualities. *Strathyre II* and *Jacquelynn Stuart* provided the best examples of the stern trawlers' capabilities known to the author. While pair trawling for herring on the Longstones grounds, the sisters took a huge haul of 315 crans. *Jacquelynn Stuart* was filled with seventy-five crans of boxed fish, but the boats managed to land all of their big catch because *Strathyre II* amazingly carried 240 crans of herring in bulk back to Eyemouth. A comparably sized traditional vessel would have been full with around 150 crans or so, and a traditional boat that could carry 240 crans would have had to have been at least 60ft long.

Strathyre II was chartered by the yard for display at the World Fishing Exhibition in Dublin in 1971. Her performance as an ambassador for Campbeltown Shipyard could scarcely have been bettered as she caught the eye of Skipper Willie Campbell of Elgin who was particularly impressed by the amount of internal space within the little steel boat compared to a wooden vessel. This was to give the yard entry into a much bigger fishing vessel market.

Strathyre II and *Jacquelynn Stuart* pair trawling together. (Courtesy Andrew Murdoch)

Strathyre II in Eyemouth with her big haul aboard. (Courtesy Andrew Murdoch)

At one time, the Campbeltown Shipyard management envisaged that the yard would series-build small stern trawlers but also had ambitions to build other types of fishing vessel. The north east of Scotland and the Moray Firth area were home to a very large fishing fleet, a considerable part of which consisted of either specialist seine net vessels or vessels which split their time between seining for white fish and pair trawling for herring. These boats were generally bigger than the ringers, measuring between 60-80ft in length and they were fishing well in the late 1960s and early 1970s. Skippers working with this class of vessel were also beginning to build new boats in steel, though these were of a traditional layout with cruiser sterns and aft wheelhouses. The first of these were the 80ft (24.38m) seiner/trawlers *Favonius* (PD17) and *Fairweather IV* (PD107) delivered by the Fairmile Construction Co. Ltd at Berwick-upon-Tweed to Peterhead owners in 1969.

The Campbeltown yard had possibly its biggest ever break in mid-1971 when it received a £200,000 order for a pair of 80ft seiner/trawlers for skippers Willie and Andrew Campbell. These orders were a great credit to the yard's management team since, following a ten per cent cut in the level of Government grant aid for new vessels, a veritable boom in new boat building came to an abrupt end and enquiries to shipyards slowed to a trickle. Andrew Campbell's *Argosy* (INS79) was the first to be launched, entering the water for the first time in June 1972 while *Ajax* (INS82) followed her down the slip in November of that year. They were built to what the yard then called its Ormsary No. 4 design but fishing history will always remember them as the first two Campbeltown 80s.

When *Argosy* and *Ajax* began fishing, they lost no time in showing what a Campbeltown 80 could do, and by 1973, they were right at the forefront of seine net fishing in Scotland. On 30 July 1973, Argosy set a record for the biggest grossing by a Scottish seiner when she landed over 700 boxes of fish at Peterhead from a six-day trip to the Ling Bank and earned £8,768. Later that year, she won the Lossie Top Catch Trophy awarded to the Lossiemouth boat that landed the highest grossing catch for a one-day trip. Argosy's winning catch, put ashore at Oban, earned £2,990 for a solitary day at sea. Meanwhile, *Ajax* had fished consistently well throughout the year and was the country's top earning seiner in 1973, earning £185,000 for her first year.

Campbeltown Shipyard picked up orders for another two 80-footers shortly after *Argosy* was launched and, by this time, the yard had also introduced its Ormsary No. 5 design. This was a 75-footer (22.86m), with her tonnage just below the 50-ton limit which meant she could be taken to sea by a skipper holding only a Second Hand (Special) Certificate instead of a Limited or Full Skipper's Certificate. In 1973, the yard added an 85ft (25.90m) design to its portfolio, correctly anticipating that seine netters were going to become still bigger. The outcome of the success of the 80-footers and the introduction of the new designs was that orders for new boats flooded into Campbeltown. At one point in October 1973, the yard had delivered five 80-footers, was about to launch a sixth and had orders for another twelve vessels – one 85-footer; five 75-footers and six 80-footers. It was launching new boats at the rate of one every six weeks.

The Campbeltown 75, 80, and 85 designs were combination seiner/trawlers and some of these boats did spend part of their time trawling, usually pair trawling. Some were delivered in time to take part in the last years of the big herring fisheries in the Minch; in later years a number of them successfully worked the white-fish pair trawl. But it was at the seine net that these vessels excelled.

Kestrel (INS121) was a consistently good performer and, in 1975, she was the top seiner operating out of Peterhead. Her £13,500 landing at Peterhead in November 1976 was a record for the port and *Kestrel* went on to become the top-earning seiner in the country that year with earnings of £261,321. *Emma Thomson* (INS100) was second top earner at Peterhead in 1978 with £294,000 and *Fidelis II* (FR319) had a remarkable £270,595 for her year in 1978 considering that she only started fishing in the spring. The champion 80-footer was, however, *Argonaut IV* (KY157), which started fishing in July 1976 and might be the champion fly-dragging seiner of all time.

Argonaut IV needed to make only one trip to break the earnings record for a Scottish seiner. After eight days at sea she landed 720 boxes at Peterhead for a grossing of £12,351. Her second trip earned £8,800 and the third wasn't far short of her record as she grossed £12,224 from 760 boxes. *Argonaut IV* took the earnings record up to £13,504 and then £13,904 later that year. In 1977, she was the top earning Scottish seiner with a staggering grossing of £434,700 for the year. In December 1978, she lifted the earnings record for a single trip up to £26,445; was again the national champion seiner with £482,700 and her skipper, David Smith, was awarded the MBE. *Argonaut IV* was the second top white-fish boat in the entire United Kingdom in 1978, narrowly beaten for top place by *CS Forrester* (H86) which grossed £489,318 and was a distant water-stern trawler more than double *Argonaut IV*'s size. *Argonaut IV* was not to be denied her half-million-pound grossing and breached the £500,000 barrier the following year when she grossed £527,582.

The 75-footers were also capable performers and *Defiance* (INS19) even managed to take *Argonaut IV*'s record grossing for a single trip away from her in autumn 1976 with a landing of 753 boxes for £14,172. *Mary Croan* (INS231) had an outstanding year in 1977 and was the top earner at Peterhead with £345,000. Ever-reliable *Kestrel* took third place for the 80-footers with £323,500, so the three top grossing seiners in Scotland were all Campbeltown built. In the meantime, big sister *Ajax* (INS168), the first of the 85-footers, had demonstrated what she could do by setting a new Scottish earnings record for a single trip by a seiner with £11,719 from 762 boxes in January 1976. She bettered that on 9 November that year when she landed 1,020 boxes at Peterhead. *Ajax* was such a good carrier that her waterline was still showing when she brought home what was then the biggest catch ever taken by a seiner. It also raised the earnings record for a single trip to £16,029.

In 1976, the Campbeltown yard began to further diversify its designs by introducing a 70-footer (21.34m) aimed at Clyde skippers and a 90-footer (27.43m) aimed at the Southern Irish market, having broken into the Irish market with a couple of 80-footers, *Marden* (D372) and *Crimson Dawn* (W119). The 70-footer had an overall length of fractionally below 70ft since vessels of 70ft and over were not allowed to bottom trawl in the Firth of Clyde. The yard also came up with a design of 87ft (26.52m) stern ramp trawler with her wheelhouse forward. By the early 1980s, Campbeltown Shipyard had introduced a Mark 2 version of the 80-footer and designs for 56-, 65- and 77-footers. The 77-footer was to a large extent the Mark 2 version of the Campbeltown 75.

From 1977 to 1984, the yard's production became extremely varied, including four 87-foot stern trawlers for the Faeroe Islands; nine 85-footers; a brace of Campbeltown 75s; three 77-footers; a 90-footer for Southern Ireland; four 70-footers; three 60-footers and seven 80-footers. One of the 60-footers, *Polonia II* (B339), was one of the most unusual fishing boats ever built at Campbeltown; a transom sterned, forward wheelhouse vessel fitted out for beam trawling and which also spent part of her time scallop dredging from the Isle of Man.

The fishing industry went through a sticky patch at the beginning of the 1980s but, by 1982, things were picking up and the new 80-footers began to show what they could do. *Auriga II* (LH449) set a new earnings record for a Scottish seiner at the end of September when she landed at North Shields after a seven-day trip and grossed £28,034 from 983 boxes. In February 1983, she was back in North Shields with 800 boxes and grossed £31,616, while her sister *Valhalla III* (LH67) had a £25,271 grossing at the port in September that year. The Moray Firth-based vessel *Karen Anne* (INS61) had a £31,500 grossing from 685 boxes at Peterhead in January 1985.

The 85-footers were also performing well. The new *Kestrel* (INS253) represented a significant change in seine netter design with her three-quarter length shelter covering in most of her working deck and her seine net winch and storage reels mounted aft of her wheelhouse. She was the third top earning seiner in the country in 1979 with £430,818 and top at Peterhead (and probably third in the country again) in 1980 with £370,385. She had a £27,561 grossing from 910 boxes at Aberdeen just after *Auriga II* set her £28,034 record.

Among the other 85-footers, *Kiloran* (INS10) had a £25,158 grossing from 820 boxes at Aberdeen in August 1983 and set a record for a seiner landing at Aberdeen when she grossed £36,258 from 963 boxes in September 1983. In the same week, *Cowrie* (INS67) had £25,000 from 820 boxes at Peterhead. Peterhead's local *Resplendent* (PD298) went pair trawling with *Spes Melior* (PD397) in 1981. In June, the team was working on the Turbot Bank and landed 800 boxes on Wednesday, 10 June for £24,000 after only two days at sea. They sailed again on the same day and were back again on the Friday with another 245 boxes worth £6,000. By 1984, *Resplendent* was back at the seine net and set a record for the heaviest landing by a local boat on 7 February, putting ashore 912 boxes for £30,139. Her next landing was one of 1,005 boxes for £19,508 and she was the top-earning seiner at Peterhead in 1984 with a grossing of £530,891 for the year.

The older vessels among the Campbeltown boats that had hit the headlines in previous years were still doing well. *Argonaut IV* had £565,000 for her year in 1982. Her £39,938 grossing at Aberdeen in January 1984 was a port record for a seiner and the boat's personal best. *Arktos II* (KY129) grossed £431,533 in 1983, while *Fidelis II* earned around £400,000 for the year and *Kiloran* (INS100) (ex-*Emma Thomson*) also passed the £400,000 mark. *Alert* (FR147) was engaged in a long-running and very successful pair-trawling partnership with the Fairmile-built *Faithful II* (PD67). In mid-1983, they were working on grounds close to home, commonly on the Turbot Bank and making multiple landings each week. At the beginning of October, they landed 760 boxes for £16,402 on the Monday and were back again three days later with another 650 boxes which sold for £10,621.

1984 was a particularly good year for the Campbeltown-built boats. During one week in mid-March, the three top grossing boats at Peterhead were all Campbeltown built: *Boy Andrew* (WK171) first with £21,263 from 1036 boxes; *Spes Melior* second with £18,110 from 612 boxes and *Ardent* (INS109) third with £16,800 from 650 boxes. In addition, *Alert* and *Faithful II* were the second-top pair-trawling team with £17,010 from 700 boxes after only five days at sea. The following week things repeated themselves. *Cowrie* was top with £16,114 from 625 boxes; *Kestrel* was second with £15,337 from 556 boxes and *Boy Andrew* was third with £14,950 from 731 boxes.

The 85ft *Boy Andrew* was the most significant vessel delivered by the yard in the period from 1977 to 1984. If any seiner might challenge *Argonaut IV*'s champion of them all' title, it was *Boy Andrew*.

Boy Andrew was delivered to top-earning Wick skipper, Norrie Bremner, though command of her passed fairly soon to his son, Andrew. The boat was built as a seiner/long liner but never fished with long lines. She spent her early years at the seine net and later diversified into pair seining and pair trawling. At the beginning of January 1983, *Boy Andrew* arrived in Peterhead after fishing over the holiday period. She landed 1,183 boxes and set a new national earnings record for a seiner with £45,071. The vessel was the top earner in 1983 with £700,600. She repeated her exploits the following year, again sailing over the holiday period and spending seven days on the Viking Bank in bad weather. Her perseverance produced 1,330 boxes of fish which sold for £58,827 and gave her a new national earnings record. She was the top seiner once again, this time with £747,000 and was champion again in 1985 with £738,805.

In 1984, *Boy Andrew*, along with the Sigbjorn Iversen-built *Nordic Prince* (BCK18), pioneered the Rockall haddock fishery by modern Scottish inshore boats. The Rockall grounds had previously been fished by larger trawlers and occasionally by great line boats but not by inshore boats. As *Nordic Prince* was rigged for trawling, *Boy Andrew* became the first seiner to work at Rockall. *Boy Andrew* made five trips to 'the Rock' between 17 August and 27 September. Four of these were eight-day trips and one lasted for eleven days. Three of the trips were underwritten by the Highlands and Islands Development Board but *Boy Andrew* made an instant success of the fishery and, in practice, the HIDB were not called upon to lay out any money at all. The five trips produced 1,177 boxes for £26,878; 815 boxes for £22,603; 790 boxes for £22,215; 1,141 boxes for £33,135 and 1,350 boxes for £30,004. Four trips were landed at Kinlochbervie and one at Wick.

Boy Andrew's success at Rockall was instrumental in the introduction of another enormously successful Campbeltown design – the 87ft seiner/trawler. In the mid-1980s there were clear warnings that fishery quotas were going to become smaller and inshore fishermen had a motivation to start fishing what to them were new and more distant grounds such as Rockall. In order to do this safely and most effectively they required large boats with big carrying capacities. To meet the anticipated demand for such boats, the Campbeltown yard introduced the 87ft design which could be fitted with a three-quarter-length shelter or be fully shelterdecked and could hold 1,600/1,800 boxes of fish against a maximum of 1,300 boxes aboard an 85-footer.

The first of the 87-footers was the fully shelterdecked *Andromeda II* (INS177) which was launched in October 1985. She had teething problems to sort out on her maiden trip in December but still performed so well as to convince her Skipper, Angus Davidson, that his new boat was nothing short of brilliant. *Andromeda II* was an extremely good sea boat and the sea conditions she could work in were a revelation. On one such day of poor conditions the new vessel managed three hauls, despite the fact that the previous *Andromeda* (INS167), a Campbeltown 80 then renamed *Arcturus* (INS167), made one haul and gave up. *Andromeda II* could shoot and haul her gear in a force 9 severe gale without any difficulty and the protection afforded by the shelterdeck meant that her skipper had no worries about losing his crew over the side.

Enquiries for 87-footers flooded into Campbeltown and these boats were the yard's biggest success since the introduction of the 80-footers. In fact, with the exception of some non-fishing vessels, the yard ended up building nothing but 87-footers and 80-footers between December 1985 and the end of 1992. In this period the yard delivered sixteen 87-footers and three 80-footers.

The 87-footers were quick to demonstrate their catching and earning abilities and pair seine fishing soon became a feature of their activities. The 80ft *Andromeda* had teamed with *Boy Andrew* to try pair seining in 1984 and established a £56,000 earnings record for this method of fishing. This was from a catch of 1,400 boxes taken on only their second trip at the pair seine. The partnership did not continue beyond this as *Boy Andrew* was going to the Rockall fishing but, the following year, *Andromeda II* paired up with her sister, *Ardent II* (INS127), and in early June took the pair seining record up to £75,673 with a landing of 1,555 boxes at Aberdeen. They beat their record on the next trip, landing 1,700 boxes at Aberdeen for £70,760. *Andromeda II* was the top earner in 1986 with £706,000. She made a particular speciality out of pair fishing and in the summer of 1988 again set records on successive trips, this time teamed up with the Johannes Kristensen-built *Liberty* (INS 153). At the end of July, the partners returned to Peterhead after a ten-day trip with 790 boxes aboard *Andromeda* and 760 aboard *Liberty*. This produced a grossing of £92,500. At the end of the pair's next trip, *Andromeda* landed 835 boxes at Aberdeen for £52,985 and *Liberty* landed 880 boxes at Peterhead for £52,399 and the team pushed the pair fishing record past the £100,000 barrier. By that time, the two boats were carrying both pair seines and pair trawls, so they could fish with either method as conditions required.

Another 87-footer which hit the heights in the second half of the 1980s was Fraserburgh Skipper Stephen Green's *Connaught II* (FR 131). *Connaught II* began fishing in November of 1986 and got off to a fine start, catching 809 boxes on her maiden trip. This catch, landed at Aberdeen, grossed £36,203. On only her third trip, she lifted the earnings record by emulating *Boy Andrew's* practice of fishing over the New Year holiday. A nine-day trip produced a catch of 1,087 boxes which sold for £59,652 on the Aberdeen market. *Connaught II* did it again in 1988, catching the first market of the year at Aberdeen with 1,015 boxes, which raised the record to £65,270.

The redoubtable 80-footers both old and new were still performing extremely well. Newcomer *Be Ready* (LK 377) began fishing in 1985 and was the highest earning white-fish boat in Shetland that year, despite fishing for only ten months of the year. Her grossing of £471,890 won the George L. Hunter Trophy for the most successful Shetland white-fish catcher over 60ft long. *Be Ready* was the third top earner in Shetland in 1986 with £467,738 for her year. She lost her title to her sister, *Donvale II* (LK 137), which made a record landing for a single trip by a Shetland boat with £25,000 from 916 boxes at Scalloway in early May and finished the year with £549,583. Second place in Shetland went to another Campbeltown-built vessel, the 85ft *Adonis* (LK 172), which earned £518,465.

The Orkney Islands also had a representative among the top earners with the 80ft trawler *Orkney Reiver* (K 49). *Orkney Reiver* grossed a remarkable £627,000 in 1985 and managed to just beat the £700,000 barrier in 1986. *Arktos II* turned in an extremely good year in 1987 when she grossed £643,000 for her year. And still among the leaders after more than ten years was *Argonaut IV*, which grossed £720,000 in 1987.

In 1986 a new 87ft *Boy Andrew* (WK 171) built at Campbeltown, paid her first visit to the Rockall grounds and the results erred on the side of the spectacular. *Boy Andrew* made three trips to 'The Rock' between 27 July and 27 August. Within this period, seventeen days of fishing time produced no less than 4,250 boxes of fish.

By the end of the 1980s, the big years were drawing to a close. Throughout the decade, white-fish quotas had generally been large enough to allow boats to make a good living, but every year the quotas became tighter. When *Andromeda* and *Liberty* set their £105,385 record in 1988 their big catch included their entire cod quota for the month of August. By 1990 quotas were shrinking at an alarming rate but there was to be one last flourish from the 87-footers. The Lochinver-based *Maranatha II* (UL 33) was delivered in time to take part in some of the best years of the Rockall fishing and, in 1990 her gross earnings for the year were just over £1 million.

The continual shrinking of white-fish quotas lead to greater interest in more distant grounds such as Rockall and, more revolutionary still, in working even more exposed North Atlantic waters on the edge of the continental shelf. The deep-water fisheries produced a whole range of unfamiliar species such as blue ling; black scabbard; deep-water red fish; grenadiers and argentines. French trawlers had been particularly proactive in developing fisheries for new species in depths from 600 to 800 fathoms on the north-east Atlantic slope, and had demonstrated that markets for these fish could be created and that deep water trawling could be economically viable. Perhaps most important of all, the deep-water fishing was quota free.

In 1994, a number of Scottish inshore vessels enjoyed some success trawling in depths between 200 and 400 fathoms. By that year, skippers had also begun building new vessels designed specifically for working in the deep water. It was necessary to create vessels with registered lengths below 80ft so as to minimise the amount of rules and regulations which would have to be complied with on the one hand, and with a maximum of working and carrying space on the other. As a result, designers came up with a completely new type of vessel. These boats were extremely high and beamy, looking like nothing that had been seen in the Scottish inshore fleet before. The vessels were all fully shelterdecked and worked their fishing gear from both main deck and shelterdeck levels. Their wheelhouses moved from the traditional aft location to a midships position so as to create more space for the installation of winches and the working of gear aft of the wheelhouse. This was a continuation of an evolutionary process which had been developing for some years and which really got underway with Campbeltown 87-footers from *Alison Kay* (LK57) onwards. The first vessel built for the deep water was *Westro* (INS20), delivered by Macduff Shipyards Ltd in 1992, though she still retained a resemblance to traditional boat design, albeit a very hefty one. The first vessel that really stood out as a completely new type was *Maranatha III* (UL33), delivered by Macduff Shipyards Ltd in 1993.

The Campbeltown yard was responsive to the needs of skippers in the ever-changing fishing industry, though an ingenious design for a mini factory trawler failed to produce any orders. This type of vessel would have had a midships engine room and two holds forward, one of which would have been a conventional chilled hold and the other a fillet store. The yard was more successful with designs for vessels adapted for deep-water trawling and won its first order for this class of vessel towards the end of 1994. This boat, *Shemarah II* (LH65), was launched in December 1995. Another deep-water trawler was ordered at the beginning of 1996. This was Fraserburgh Skipper Sandy West's *Steadfast IV* (FR443), launched on 30 October, 1996 and the last fishing boat built by Campbeltown Shipyard.

The boatbuilding industry has always had its ups and downs, reflecting the changing fortunes of the fishing industry, but by 1990, the boatyards were facing a crisis like nothing previously seen in modern times and several had already closed down. There were a number of reasons for this and these, piled one after another on the struggling industry, brought about its widespread demise.

By 1990 grant aid on which much new vessel construction had depended had become exceedingly scarce. Under the EEC multi-annual guidance plan, the British white-fish fleet was twenty per cent over capacity, so the immediate EEC emphasis was on taking tonnage out of the fleet and not on building new vessels. The Boatbuilders' Association pressed in vain for grant aid to allow a limited vessel renewal scheme, coupled with a decommissioning scheme to take boats out of the fleet. Other EEC nations were already operating decommissioning schemes, financed largely by the EEC, but the British Government proved very slow to adopt such measures which were not introduced until 1993.

Restrictive licensing also began to create major problems for the boatyards. In 1984, there were fears that this would lead to serious difficulties for the construction of new boats, but initially this did not prove to be the case. As time wore on, however, licences became scarcer and rules regarding their transfer and aggregation became tighter. By 1990, the obtaining of sufficient licence capacity to build a new vessel had become a significant problem and the cost of acquisition of additional licence capacity had turned into a considerable deterrent to any skipper who was contemplating building a new boat.

Diversification at Campbeltown (1). This is the wellboat *Solea*. (Courtesy John M. Addison)

Diversification at Campbeltown (2). This is the ferry *Thorsvoe*. (Courtesy John M. Addison)

Last of the breed – *Crear* tied up in Buckie. (Peter Drummond)

White-fish quotas continued to shrink and, in 1992, the introduction of compulsory tie-up periods made the economics of both fishing and new boat building still worse.

In the late 1980s and early 1990s, Campbeltown Shipyard diversified its boatbuilding activities in order to survive. In this period the yard built a handful of fishing boats; the 110ft wellboat *Solea* and the 46ft workboats *Fishnish* and *Fyne Lass* for the fish farming industry; a ferry called *Thorsvoe* for Orkney Islands Council and the 100ft floating restaurant *Debra Rose*. The shipyard also built sections of a tug under sub-contract to McTay Marine. The yard went on to do more steel fabrication work for the fish-farming industry but it was by then postponing the inevitable end. The final blow which hit Campbeltown Shipyard, and indeed all remaining British yards, was in the mid-1990s when fishing-boat orders began to flow to overseas builders.

It was nothing new for British fishermen to build vessels in Continental yards, though this was a trend which had accelerated in the 1970s. Towards the end of that decade, increasing numbers of orders for new boats went to Norwegian shipyards due to the availability of low-interest loans to assist with vessel construction in that country. A number of these orders were for purse seiners for the pelagic industry. The Campbeltown yard did not build pursers but the Norwegian yards also picked up orders for a handful of seiner/trawlers and small stern trawlers which did place them in competition with Campbeltown Shipyard.

By 1983, there was an issue between Campbeltown Shipyard and the Johannes Kristensen yard in Hvide Sande in Denmark. The 80ft and 85ft seiner/trawlers built by Kristensens were aimed at the Scottish market and were direct competitors of the Campbeltown 80ft and 85ft designs. Things came to something of a head in 1983 when Campbeltown Shipyard quoted £767,000 to try to win the order for *Liberty* and lost out to Kristensens whose quote had come in at £578,000. The Danish yard was suspected of using two sets of

Desolation at Campbeltown. The silent and deserted Campbeltown Shipyard after closure. From above to opposite: the house which accommodated the yard's offices; the main yard buildings from the landward side; and the yard from the seaward side. (Sam Henderson)

unemployment subsidies to compete unfairly with British yards, though the management at Kristensens denied that they were taking advantage of these schemes. Certainly, there were times when the rate of exchange of the pound sterling and the Danish kroner was very favourable to the building of vessels in Denmark, and this did give Kristensens a temporary advantage in the new-vessel market. It is also beyond question that Kristensens built very fine boats. A Campbeltown 87 and a Kristensens 85-footer teamed up made a formidable fish-catching combination, as *Andromeda II* and *Liberty* had demonstrated.

Competition from foreign yards moved into a new dimension from the mid-1990s onwards. Orders continued to go to Norwegian, Danish and Dutch yards. Polish yards with very low labour costs and European Union aid also began to win a share of the market but the biggest concern for the remaining British yards was the sheer number of orders which began to go to Spain.

In Spain, regional grants were available to encourage owners to build in Spanish yards. When these were combined with European Union grants, it was possible to obtain a subsidy of over fifty per cent of the cost of a new vessel. The first Spanish yard to break into the British market was Astilleros Armon of Navia that delivered its first boat for this country, the Channel Islands crabber *Our Hazel* (GU171), in 1994. By the end of that year, Armon had four orders for the United Kingdom and, most significantly, it was picking up orders for vessels designed for deep water trawling from Scottish owners. It delivered its first vessel to Scotland, the *Crusader* (BCK16), in January 1995.

It was widely perceived among the remaining British shipbuilders that the grant assistance available to foreign yards was distorting the market for new vessels and placing the continental yards at an unfair advantage. When the Moodie family, the owners of *Shemarah II*, had her built in Campbeltown, they placed the order with the Campbeltown yard partly out of loyalty to Scottish shipyards notwithstanding that the vessel could have been built abroad at a lower price. However, harsh economics dictated that few skippers could afford this kind of loyalty. The Spanish yards in particular were giving skippers a product they wanted i.e. vessels able to trawl in the deep water, at a price they could afford. This could produce only one outcome. Any skipper faced with the choice between building a new vessel which should help him to move with the times and keep him in business on the one hand and not building at all and possibly going out of business on the other, was going to build in Spain.

In 1995, the Lithgow group acquired the Jones Buckie Shipyard and also the Herd & Mackenzie yard at Buckie, when even these long-established and highly reputable builders were on the point of closure due to the state of the industry. It was at one time intended that Lithgows would have vessel hulls built at Campbeltown, and that these would be fitted out at Buckie. In practice, little was done under this scheme. Campbeltown Shipyard delivered its last vessel of all, a 113ft wellboat/dry cargo vessel named *Crear* in 1997. After that, the yard built a couple of feed barges for the fish-farming industry and the hull of a Caledonian MacBrayne ferry which was fitted out at Buckie. The yard also did some more steel-fabrication work and some repair and maintenance work on fishing boats but the end had come and the yard was mothballed in 1997. The last of the workforce were paid off in November of that year.

When this book was completed, the site of Campbeltown Shipyard still belonged to Lithgows but a vacant site was all that remained. The buildings had been demolished and the yard, which had done so well for many years, is now gone. Many of its fishing vessels are also gone – the 2003 decommissioning scheme was very hard on Campbeltown-built boats. Ten of these had gone for scrapping by September, including five 87-footers which had years of service left in them. Even more symptomatic of the destruction of the Scottish fishing fleet by European Union-driven decommissioning was the scrapping of *Steadfast IV* when only seven years old.

Decommissioning, restricted days at sea and shrinking quotas have left the Scottish fleet a shadow of its former self. However, by the middle of the first decade of the twenty-first century, things were beginning to look up for the remaining vessels, including several survivors of the boats built by Campbeltown Shipyard.

Opportunus III (PD96), built at Campbeltown as the seiner *Surmount* (BCK98) in 1974 began twin-rig trawling from Peterhead under skipper James Buchan in 2002. She fished so well at the twin rig as to finance the building of a 20-m replacement vessel which was ordered in 2006. The new boat, *Opportunus IV* (PD96) was built by Karstensens Shipyard at Skagen in Denmark and delivered at the end of July 2007.

Boy Andrew (WK170) fishing as a single-boat seiner from Scrabster, took her annual earnings up to just over £1 million in 2006, even though she was by then twenty years old. *Castlewood* (FR216), built in 1978 as *Kestrel* (INS253), remains one of the top-earning boats in the industry, pair-trawling with the Buckie-built *Ryanwood* (FR307). *Castlewood* has also earned over £1 million for a year's work in the new century and, on 16 January 2007, the boats set a new record for a pair team when they grossed £118,700 from a landing of 1,448 boxes at Peterhead. *Castlewood* might be approaching thirty years of age but she is still a record breaker. With boats still turning in performances like this, the fishing industry will long remember the fishing boats of Campbeltown Shipyard.

A-Z of Fishing Boats of Campbeltown Shipyard

There follows a comprehensive list of fishing vessels built by Campbeltown Shipyard. Under the heading 'Alterations' on each boat's page, we have not tried to record every change which was made to these boats but have instead confined ourselves to major modifications which significantly affect the external appearance of a vessel, though we have also included all changes of main engine known to us. The information, while believed to be correct, is not guaranteed to be absolutely accurate. The objective is to record for posterity what the fishing boats of Campbeltown Shipyard were like and this book is not intended to be a substitute for any official source of information regarding fishing vessels.

The information contained in this book is, to the best of the authors' knowledge and belief, correct to 31 July 2008.

ADONIS LK371

Two views of *Adonis* at Acanthus (FR138). (Peter Drummond)

Year Built: 1975 **Yard No.:** 24 **Call Sign:** 2HNS
Principal dimensions in metres:
O/Length: 22.86 **R/Length:** 21.31 **Breadth:** 6.40 **Depth:** 2.29
Engine Make: Kelvin TBSC8 **HP:** 500
Deck layout: Open deck whaleback
Type of stern: Cruiser
First owners: M. Stewart & Partners, Symbister, Shetland

Vessel Renamed	Renumbered	Year
Adonis	BCK123	1985
Curlew	BCK123	1986
Acanthus	FR138	1990

Alterations: Gutting shelter later extended to three-quarter-length shelter 532HP Kelvin
Status: Decommissioned 2002

ADONIS LK172

Adonis. (Courtesy Ian Leask)

Year Built: 1985　　**Yard No.:** 70　　**Call Sign:** GFCY
Principal dimensions in metres:
O/Length: 25.90　　**R/Length:** 23.93　　**Breadth:** 7.15　　**Depth:** 3.08
Engine Make: Deutz SBA12M816U　　**HP:** 671
Deck layout: Three-quarter-length shelter
Type of stern: Cruiser
First owners: D. Cumming & Partners, Burra, Shetland

Vessel Renamed	Renumbered	Year
–	–	–

Alterations: Lengthened 2.55m aft and stern changed to transom
Full shelterdeck
Status: Capsized and sank after engine room fire west-north-west of Foula on 22 June, 1994. All crew picked up safely by *Endeavour* (LK173).

AJAX INS82

Two views of *Ajax* as *Argosy* (INS82). (Peter Drummond)

Year Built: 1972　　**Yard No.:** 12　　**Call Sign:** MJUK
Principal dimensions in metres:
O/Length: 24.36　　**R/Length:** 22.53　　**Breadth:** 6.71　　**Depth:** 2.84
Engine Make: Caterpillar D346TA　　**HP:** 480
Deck layout: Open deck whaleback
Type of stern: Cruiser
First owners: W. Campbell, Elgin & Partners

Vessel Renamed	Renumbered	Year
Argosy	INS82	1975

Alterations: Gutting shelter
565HP Caterpillar
Status: Decommissioned 2002

AJAX INS168

Ajax in Peterhead Bay.
(Peter Drummond)

Ajax at Scrabster.
(Courtesy John M. Addison)

Year Built: 1975   **Yard No.:** 26   **Call Sign:** 2IFT
Principal dimensions in metres:
O/Length: 25.70   **R/Length:** 24.15   **Breadth:** 7.23   **Depth:** 3.11
Engine Make: Caterpillar D379TA   **HP:** 565
Deck layout: Whaleback gutting shelter
Type of stern: Cruiser
First owners: W. Campbell, Elgin

Vessel Renamed	Renumbered	Year
–	–	–

Alterations: –
Status: Decommissioned 2003

ALERT FR147

Alert as *Sunlight* (PD187). (Courtesy David Linkie)

Year Built: 1974 **Yard No.:** 19 **Call Sign:** 2FIN
Principal dimensions in metres:
O/Length: 24.35 **R/Length:** 22.52 **Breadth:** 6.71 **Depth:** 2.83
Engine Make: Kelvin TBSC8 **HP:** 500
Deck layout: Open deck whaleback
Type of stern: Cruiser
First owners: Ian Smith, Peterhead & Partners

Vessel Renamed	Renumbered	Year
Sunlight	PD187	1984
Boy Andrew	PD136	1988
Tea Rose	K136	1990
Tea Rose	–	1995
Tea Rose	N216	2001

Alterations: Gutting shelter
750HP Caterpillar
Three-quarter-length shelter
811HP Caterpillar
Status: Still fishing

ALISON KAY LK57

Alison Kay leaving Peterhead. (Peter Drummond)

Alison Kay at sea. (Peter Drummond)

Year Built: 1988   **Yard No.:** 82   **Call Sign:** MKGG3
Principal dimensions in metres:
O/Length: 26.88   **R/Length:** 24.39   **Breadth:** 7.50   **Depth:** 3.66
Engine Make: Deutz SBA12M816   **HP:** 775
Deck layout: Full shelterdeck
Type of stern: Transom
First owners: J.D. Anderson & Partners, Skerries, Shetland

Vessel Renamed	Renumbered	Year
Mizpah LK	LK57	1999

Alterations: 775HP Caterpillar
Status: Still fishing

ALKAID UL257

Alkaid. (Peter Drummond)

Alkaid as *Pleiades* (BF576). (Peter Drummond)

Year Built: 1982 **Yard No.:** 61 **Call Sign:** MBCZ5
Principal dimensions in metres:
O/Length: 18.25 **R/Length:** 16.40 **Breadth:** 6.58 **Depth:** 3.75
Engine Make: Kelvin TASC8 **HP:** 440
Deck layout: Three-quarter-length shelter
Type of stern: Transom
First owners: G.S. Main, Hopeman & Partners

Vessel Renamed	Renumbered	Year
Alkaid	INS256	1993
Pleiades	BF576	1996
Copious	LK985	1999
Copious	WY170	2004

Alterations: –
Status: Still fishing

ANDROMEDA INS167

Andromeda as *Alert* (INS 55). (Peter Drummond)

Year Built: 1975 **Yard No.:** 22 **Call Sign:** 2FYV
Principal dimensions in metres:
O/Length: 24.38 **R/Length:** 22.53 **Breadth:** 6.72 **Depth:** 2.84
Engine Make: Caterpillar D379TA **HP:** 565
Deck layout: Whaleback gutting shelter
Type of stern: Cruiser
First owners: J. Campbell, Lossiemouth & Partners

Vessel Renamed	Renumbered	Year
Arcturus	INS167	1985
Alert	INS55	1999

Alterations: –
Status: Decommissioned 2002

ANDROMEDA II INS177

Two views of *Andromeda II*. (Peter Drummond)

Year Built: 1985 **Yard No.:** 72 **Call Sign:** GFWQ
Principal dimensions in metres:
O/Length: 26.68 **R/Length:** 24.36 **Breadth:** 7.51 **Depth:** 3.69
Engine Make: Callesen 5-427-EOT **HP:** 575
Deck layout: Full shelterdeck
Type of stern: Transom
First owners: A. Davidson, Hopeman & Partners

Vessel Renamed **Renumbered** **Year**
— — —

Alterations: –
Status: Decommissioned 2003

AQUARIAN CN42

Aquarian. (Courtesy Lachie Paterson)

Year Built: 1971   **Yard No.:** 6   **Call Sign:** MTOM
Principal dimensions in metres:
O/Length: 15.21   **R/Length:** 14.20   **Breadth:** 4.91   **Depth:** 1.83
Engine Make: Dorman 6LEM   **HP:** 142
Deck layout: Open deck
Type of stern: Transom
First owners: A. Galbraith, Campbeltown

Vessel Renamed	Renumbered	Year
Aquarian	BF281	1977

Alterations: 280HP Kelvin
370HP Kelvin
Status: Began taking in water and sank 10 miles off Kinlochbervie on 31 March 1983. All crew picked up safely by *Coral Strand II* (BF24).

AQUARIUS INS222

Aquarius. (Courtesy Lachie Paterson)

Year Built: 1975 **Yard No.:** 23 **Call Sign:** GUQK
Principal dimensions in metres:
O/Length: 24.38 **R/Length:** 22.53 **Breadth:** 6.72 **Depth:** 2.84
Engine Make: Caterpillar D346TA **HP:** 480
Deck layout: Whaleback gutting shelter
Type of stern: Cruiser
First owners: C. Scott & Partners, Lossiemouth

Vessel Renamed	Renumbered	Year
Fertile	INS222	1981

Alterations: –
Status: Began taking in water and sank while fishing around 180 miles north-east of Aberdeen on 23 April 1981. All crew picked up safely by oil rig standby vessel *Grampian Defender*.

ARDENT II INS127

Ardent II seen both inward and outward bound. (Peter Drummond)

Year Built: 1986 **Yard No.:** 73 **Call Sign:** GFWP
Principal dimensions in metres:
O/Length: 26.70 **R/Length:** 24.36 **Breadth:** 7.50 **Depth:** 4.25
Engine Make: Callesen 5-427-EOT **HP:** 575
Deck layout: Full shelterdeck
Type of stern: Transom
First owners: J. McPherson, Hopeman & Partners

Vessel Renamed	Renumbered	Year
–	–	–

Alterations: –
Status: Still fishing

ARGONAUT IV KY157

Argonaut IV. (Courtesy Peter Brady)

Argonaut IV with her three-quarter shelter and Irish registration. (Courtesy David Linkie)

Year Built: 1976   **Yard No.:** 32   **Call Sign:** 2LEJ
Principal dimensions in metres:
O/Length: 24.36   **R/Length:** 22.52   **Breadth:** 6.74   **Depth:** 2.84
Engine Make: Caterpillar D379TA   **HP:** 565
Deck layout: Whaleback gutting shelter
Type of stern: Cruiser
First owners: D. & R. Smith, Anstruther

Vessel Renamed	Renumbered	Year
Argonaut IV	DA22	2003

Alterations: 565hp Caterpillar, and three-quarter-length shelter
Status: Still fishing

ARGOSY INS79

Argosy as *Valkyrie* (INS79). (Courtesy Peter Brady)

Year Built: 1972   **Yard No.:** 11   **Call Sign:** MVUU
Principal dimensions in metres:
O/Length: 24.35   **R/Length:** 22.52   **Breadth:** 6.71   **Depth:** 2.84
Engine Make: Caterpillar D346TA   **HP:** 480
Deck layout: Open deck whaleback
Type of stern: Cruiser
First owners: A. Campbell, Lossiemouth & Partners

Vessel Renamed	Renumbered	Year
Swiftsure	INS79	1975
Valkyrie	INS79	1979

Alterations: Gutting shelter
565HP Caterpillar, initially derated to 480HP, then uprated back to 565HP
Status: Ran aground on Shetland island of Bressay and thereafter sank on 13 March 1991. All crew picked up safely from liferaft by pair seining partner *Rosemary* (INS189).

ARGYLL INS217

Argyll. (Courtesy David Linkie)

Year Built: 1982   **Yard No.:** 62   **Call Sign:** MBLV6
Principal dimensions in metres:
O/Length: 24.30   **R/Length:** 21.74   **Breadth:** 7.17   **Depth:** 3.48
Engine Make: Deutz SBA8M816R   **HP:** 554
Deck layout: Whaleback gutting shelter
Type of stern: Cruiser
First owners: B. Walker, Burghead & Partners

Vessel Renamed	Renumbered	Year
Roise Catriona	T100	2001

Alterations: Three-quarter-length shelter
Status: Still fishing

ARKH ANGELL K616

Arkh-Angell. (Peter Drummond)

Year Built: 1990 **Yard No.:** 88 **Call Sign:** MMQL8
Principal dimensions in metres:
O/Length: 26.64 **R/Length:** 23.70 **Breadth:** 7.50 **Depth:** 3.67
Engine Make: Deutz SBA12816R **HP:** 795
Deck layout: Full shelterdeck
Type of stern: Transom
First owners: K. Bain, Kirkwall, Orkney

Vessel Renamed	Renumbered	Year
–	–	–

Alterations: 800HP Caterpillar
Status: Still fishing

ARKTOS II KY129

Arktos II. (Courtesy Peter Brady)

Arktos II with her three-quarter shelter. (Courtesy Peter Brady)

Year Built: 1979   **Yard No.:** 45   **Call Sign:** 2YMH
Principal dimensions in metres:
O/Length: 24.36   **R/Length:** 22.55   **Breadth:** 6.82   **Depth:** 2.83
Engine Make: Caterpillar D379TA   **HP:** 565
Deck layout: Whaleback gutting shelter
Type of stern: Cruiser
First owners: J.C. Murray, Anstruther & Partners

Vessel Renamed	**Renumbered**	**Year**
–	–	–

Alterations: Three-quarter-length shelter
660HP Caterpillar
Status: Sank 75 miles west of Stavanger, Norway, 1 March 2003. All crew picked up safely by Royal Norwegian Air Force helicopter.

AURIGA II LH449

Auriga II. (Courtesy Peter Brady)

Auriga II as Arcane (INS171). (Peter Drummond)

Auriga II as *White Wings* (PD362). (Peter Drummond)

Year Built: 1981 **Yard No.:** 58 **Call Sign:** MASY7
Principal dimensions in metres:
O/Length: 24.30 **R/Length:** 21.74 **Breadth:** 7.17 **Depth:** 3.48
Engine Make: Callesen 5-427-EOT **HP:** 575
Deck layout: Whaleback gutting shelter
Type of stern: Cruiser
First owners: J.Vanko, St Abbs & Partners

Vessel Renamed	Renumbered	Year
Auriga II	INS171	1989
Arcane	INS171	1989
White Wings	PD362	1999
Arcane	N907	2002

Alterations: –
Status: Still fishing

BE READY LK377

Be Ready.
(Courtesy Ian Leask)

Year Built: 1985   **Yard No.:** 69   **Call Sign:** GDZN
Principal dimensions in metres:
O/Length: 24.54   **R/Length:** 22.47   **Breadth:** 7.23   **Depth:** 3.32
Engine Make: Deutz SBA8M816R   **HP:** 554
Deck layout: Three-quarter-length shelter
Type of stern: Cruiser
First owners: T. Fullerton, Burra, Shetland

Vessel Renamed	Renumbered	Year
Be Ready	–	2000
Be Ready	G463	2001
Celtic Buccaneer	DA58	2005

Alterations: Full shelterdeck
New wheelhouse
554HP Cummins
Status: Decommissioned 2008

BENAIAH II B350

Benaiah II as Discovery (BF268). (Peter Drummond)

Year Built: 1981　　**Yard No.:** 55　　**Call Sign:** GBYX
Principal dimensions in metres:
O/Length: 21.24　　**R/Length:** 19.70　　**Breadth:** 6.71　　**Depth:** 2.45
Engine Make: Kelvin TBSC8　　**HP:** 500
Deck layout: Open deck whaleback
Type of stern: Transom
First owners: D. Jones, Annalong, N. Ireland

Vessel Renamed	Renumbered	Year
Discovery	BF268	1994

Alterations: Gutting shelter later extended to three-quarter-length shelter
Lengthened 2.14m
535HP Kelvin
Status: Still fishing

BOY ANDREW WK171

Boy Andrew as *Opportune* (WK171). (Peter Drummond)

Opportune with her new wheelhouse. (Sam Henderson)

Year Built: 1979   **Yard No.:** 44   **Call Sign:** 2WKN
Principal dimensions in metres:
O/Length: 25.90   **R/Length:** 24.14   **Breadth:** 7.22   **Depth:** 3.10
Engine Make: Mirrlees Blackstone ESL6MK2   **HP:** 650
Deck layout: Full shelterdeck
Type of stern: Cruiser
First owners: N. Bremner & Partners, Wick

Vessel Renamed	Renumbered	Year
Opportune	WK171	1986

Alterations: Shelter reduced to three-quarter length
New wheelhouse
650HP Callesen
Status: Still fishing

BOY ANDREW WK170

Two views of *Boy Andrew* at Scrabster. (Sam Henderson)

Year Built: 1986 **Yard No.:** 74 **Call Sign:** GGPE
Principal dimensions in metres:
O/Length: 26.61 **R/Length:** 24.61 **Breadth:** 7.50 **Depth:** 4.25
Engine Make: Callesen 6-427-FOT **HP:** 690
Deck layout: Three-quarter-length shelter
Type of stern: Cruiser
First owners: Bremner Fishing Co. Ltd, Wick

Vessel Renamed	Renumbered	Year
–	–	–

Alterations: –
Status: Still fishing

BRERETON INS97

Brereton. (Courtesy Peter Brady)

Brereton as *Advance II* (INS77). (Peter Drummond)

Year Built: 1987 **Yard No.:** 78 **Call Sign:** MZNA6
Principal dimensions in metres:
O/Length: 26.54 **R/Length:** 24.36 **Breadth:** 7.50 **Depth:** 3.63
Engine Make: Callesen 5-427-EOT **HP:** 575
Deck layout: Full shelterdeck
Type of stern: Transom
First owners: T. Martin, Lossiemouth & Partners

Vessel Renamed	Renumbered	Year
Valhalla IV	LH184	1989
Advance II	INS77	1999

Alterations: –
Status: Still fishing

BUDDING ROSE PD418

Budding Rose outward bound from Peterhead as seen from the end of Albert Quay. (Peter Drummond)

Budding Rose outward bound from Peterhead as seen from the South Breakwater. (Peter Drummond)

Year Built: 1990 **Yard No.:** 87 **Call Sign:** MMEV2
Principal dimensions in metres:
O/Length: 24.54 **R/Length:** 22.50 **Breadth:** 6.50 **Depth:** 3.05
Engine Make: Deutz SBA12M816U **HP:** 721
Deck layout: Three-quarter-length shelter
Type of stern: Transom
First owners: P. Bruce & Partners, Peterhead

Vessel Renamed	**Renumbered**	**Year**
–	–	–

Alterations: –
Status: Still fishing

CAVALIER INS109

Two views of *Cavalier* as *Atlantis* (INS109) outward bound from Peterhead. (Peter Drummond)

Year Built: 1973   **Yard No.:** 14   **Call Sign:** 2CAF
Principal dimensions in metres:
O/Length: 24.36   **R/Length:** 22.53   **Breadth:** 6.71   **Depth:** 2.84
Engine Make: Mirrlees Blackstone ERS6MGR   **HP:** 495
Deck layout: Open deck whaleback
Type of stern: Cruiser
First owners: J. McPherson, Hopeman & Partners

Vessel Renamed	Renumbered	Year
Ardent	INS109	1981
Atlantis	INS109	1986

Alterations: Gutting shelter
Status: Decommissioned 2002

CHALLENGER II PD212

Challenger II. (Courtesy John M. Addison)

A work-stained *Challenger II* as *Fertile* (PD353). (Peter Drummond)

Year Built: 1977   **Yard No.:** 37   **Call Sign:** 2PXQ
Principal dimensions in metres:
O/Length: 25.91   **R/Length:** 24.14   **Breadth:** 7.22   **Depth:** 3.11
Engine Make: Mirrlees Blackstone ESL6MGR   **HP:** 600
Deck layout: Whaleback gutting shelter
Type of stern: Cruiser
First owners: A. Strachan & W. Innes, Peterhead

Vessel Renamed	Renumbered	Year
Fertile	PD353	1988
Helenus	FR421	1994
Ryanwood	FR421	1996

Alterations: –
Status: Decommissioned 2002

CONNAUGHT II FR131

Connaught II. (Courtesy Ian Leask)

Connaught II as *Starlight Rays* (PD230). (Peter Drummond)

Year Built: 1986 **Yard No.:** 75 **Call Sign:** GHVD
Principal dimensions in metres:
O/Length: 26.61 **R/Length:** 24.49 **Breadth:** 7.50 **Depth:** 4.29
Engine Make: B & W Alpha ST23L-KVO **HP:** 775
Deck layout: Three-quarter-length shelter
Type of stern: Transom
First owners: S. Green, Fraserburgh & Partners

Vessel Renamed	Renumbered	Year
Connaught	LK171	1993
Starlight Rays	PD230	1999

Alterations: Full shelterdeck
Status: Decommissioned 2003

COWRIE INS67

Cowrie. (Courtesy Peter Brady)

Cowrie as *Supreme* (INS276). (Peter Drummond)

Cowrie as *Morning Star* (PD966). (Peter Drummond)

Year Built: 1983 **Yard No.:** 64 **Call Sign:** MCEU5
Principal dimensions in metres:
O/Length: 26.00 **R/Length:** 24.30 **Breadth:** 7.25 **Depth:** 3.10
Engine Make: Callesen 6-427-EOT **HP:** 575
Deck layout: Whaleback gutting shelter
Type of stern: Cruiser
First owners: S. Edwards, Whitehills & Partners

Vessel Renamed	Renumbered	Year
Supreme	INS276	1993
Morning Star	PD966	2000

Alterations: –
Status: Decommissioned 2003

CRIMSON ARROW CN30

Two views of *Crimson Arrow* as *Star of David* (BA258) leaving Girvan. Note the harpoon gun used for catching basking sharks on her bow. (Peter Drummond)

Year Built: 1970   **Yard No.:** 1   **Call Sign:** MOYF
Principal dimensions in metres:
O/Length: 15.06   **R/Length:** 14.29   **Breadth:** 4.91   **Depth:** 1.92
Engine Make: Dorman 6LEM   **HP:** 142
Deck layout: Open deck
Type of stern: Transom
First owners: J. Macdonald, Campbeltown

Vessel Renamed	Renumbered	Year
Dawn Carol	CN30	1974
Dawn Carol	BA258	1978
Star of David	BA258	1991

Alterations: 180HP Volvo
Gutting shelter (later removed)
Status: Decommissioned 1993

CRIMSON DAWN W119

Crimson Dawn as Ocean Reaper II (FR273). (Peter Drummond)

Year Built: 1976   **Yard No.:** 30   **Call Sign:** EIMD
Principal dimensions in metres:
O/Length: 24.68   **Length BP:** 21.45   **Breadth:** 6.72   **M/Depth:** 3.35
Engine Make: British Polar SF 13 RSF   **HP:** 580
Deck layout: Open deck whaleback
Type of stern: Cruiser
First owners: S. O'Driscoll, Waterford, S. Ireland

Vessel Renamed	Renumbered	Year
Crimson Dawn	N307	1988
Crystal Sea	N307	1988
Crystal Sea	FR366	1994
Harvest Moon	FR366	1994
Ocean Reaper 11	FR273	1995
Morning Star	LH444	1996

Alterations: Three-quarter-length shelter
554HP Deutz
Status: Decommissioned 2002

CRYSTAL RIVER B346

Crystal River. (Courtesy Peter Brady)

Crystal River with her shelterdeck and Banff registration. (Peter Drummond)

Year Built: 1981 **Yard No.:** 54 **Call Sign:** GBWH
Principal dimensions in metres:
O/Length: 21.24 **R/Length:** 19.70 **Breadth:** 6.71 **Depth:** 2.45
Engine Make: Kelvin TBSC8 **HP:** 500
Deck layout: Open deck whaleback
Type of stern: Transom
First owners: R. Jones, Kilkeel & A. Robinson, Annalong, N. Ireland

Vessel Renamed	Renumbered	Year
Crystal River	BF32	1985
Eshcol	BCK65	1993

Alterations: Full shelterdeck
624HP Caterpillar
Status: Still fishing

DEFIANCE INS19

Above: Defiance as Robian (FR29). (Peter Drummond)

Left: Defiance. (Courtesy John M. Addison)

Year Built: 1975   **Yard No.:** 25   **Call Sign:** 2JAM
Principal dimensions in metres:
O/Length: 22.87   **R/Length:** 21.31   **Breadth:** 6.40   **Depth:** 2.28
Engine Make: Caterpillar D346TA   **HP:** 480
Deck layout: Whaleback gutting shelter
Type of stern: Cruiser
First owners: W. More, Burghead & Partners

Vessel Renamed	Renumbered	Year
Defiance	FR29	1986
Robian	FR29	1986
Active	INS272	1991

Alterations: Three-quarter-length shelter
498HP Caterpillar
Status: Sank after collision with pair seining partner *Supreme* (INS276) 70 miles off the Norwegian coast 13 October 1992. Both vessels lost but all crew picked up safely from life rafts by Norwegian rescue helicopter.

DEFIANT LK371

Defiant. (Courtesy Ian Leask)

Year Built: 1987   **Yard No.:** 79   **Call Sign:** MHGC3
Principal dimensions in metres:
O/Length: 26.61   **R/Length:** 24.49   **Breadth:** 7.50   **Depth:** 4.29
Engine Make: Caterpillar D3508TA   **HP:** 775
Deck layout: Full shelterdeck
Type of stern: Transom
First owners: M. Stewart & Partners, Shetland

Vessel Renamed	Renumbered	Year
—	—	—

Alterations: 790HP Caterpillar
775hp Deutz
Status: Still fishing

DONVALE II LK137

Donvale II. (Peter Drummond)

Year Built: 1985   **Yard No.:** 71   **Call Sign:** GFKX
Principal dimensions in metres:
O/Length: 24.35   **R/Length:** 22.39   **Breadth:** 7.21   **Depth:** 3.25
Engine Make: Kelvin TGSC8   **HP:** 650
Deck layout: Three-quarter-length shelter
Type of stern: Transom
First owners: J. Fullerton & Partners, Shetland

Vessel Renamed	Renumbered	Year
–	–	–

Alterations: 650HP Caterpillar
Full shelterdeck
Status: Decommissioned 2003

DRAIOCHT NA MARA D501

Draiocht na Mara. (Courtesy Peter Brady)

Year Built: 1980 **Yard No.:** 48 **Call Sign:** EIWG
Principal dimensions in metres:
O/Length: 27.44 **Length BP:** 23.63 **Breadth:** 7.21 **M/Depth:** 3.75
Engine Make: B & W Alpha 408-26VO **HP:** 800
Deck layout: Three-quarter-length shelter
Type of stern: Transom
First owners: K. O'Driscoll, Castletownbere, S. Ireland

Vessel Renamed	Renumbered	Year
–	–	–

Alterations: Full shelterdeck
Status: Ceased fishing and laid up in Dingle. Scrapping anticipated 2008/2009

EMMA THOMSON INS100

Two views of *Emma Thomson* as *Oceanic* (INS100). (Peter Drummond)

Year Built: 1975 **Yard No.:** 28 **Call Sign:** 21BL
Principal dimensions in metres:
O/Length: 24.36 **R/Length:** 22.53 **Breadth:** 6.71 **Depth:** 2.84
Engine Make: Caterpillar D379TA **HP:** 565
Deck layout: Whaleback gutting shelter
Type of stern: Cruiser
First owners: A.Thomson, Lossiemouth & Partners

Vessel Renamed	Renumbered	Year
Kiloran	INS100	1980
Oceanic	INS100	1983
Mamre Oaks	FR57	1997

Alterations: Three-quarter-length shelter
Stern changed to transom
561HP Caterpillar
Status: Decommissioned 2002

ENDEAVOUR LK173

Endeavour. (Courtesy Ian Leask)

Endeavour as *Constant Friend III* (PD83). (Sam Henderson)

Year Built: 1988   **Yard No.:** 83   **Call Sign:** MKJH5
Principal dimensions in metres:
O/Length: 26.88   **R/Length:** 24.38   **Breadth:** 7.50   **Depth:** 4.25
Engine Make: Mirrlees Blackstone ESL5MK2   **HP:** 830
Deck layout: Full shelterdeck
Type of stern: Transom
First owners: B. Morrison & Partners, Shetland

Vessel Renamed	Renumbered	Year
Constant Friend III	PD83	1998

Alterations: 830HP Stork Wärtsilä
Status: Decommissioned 2003

FALCON INS117

Falcon. (Courtesy John M. Addison)

Falcon showing her Fraserburgh registration. (Courtesy Ian Leask)

Year Built: 1974   **Yard No.:** 17   **Call Sign:** 2DOK
Principal dimensions in metres:
O/Length: 22.85   **R/Length:** 21.29   **Breadth:** 6.43   **Depth:** 2.28
Engine Make: Caterpillar D346TA   **HP:** 480
Deck layout: Open deck whaleback
Type of stern: Cruiser
First owners: G. Sutherland, Hopeman & Partners

Vessel Renamed	Renumbered	Year
Falcon	FR119	1990
Dunkeld	FR261	1996
Random Harvest III	D672	2000

Alterations: Gutting shelter
480HP Caterpillar
480HP Caterpillar (Second new engine)
Status: Decommissioned 2008

FEAR NOT INS197

Fear Not outward bound from Peterhead. (Peter Drummond)

Fear Not seen just after leaving Peterhead Bay. (Peter Drummond)

Year Built: 1976 **Yard No.:** 33 **Call Sign:** 2LVF
Principal dimensions in metres:
O/Length: 24.38 **R/Length:** 22.53 **Breadth:** 6.70 **Depth:** 2.83
Engine Make: Caterpillar D379TA **HP:** 565
Deck layout: Whaleback gutting shelter
Type of stern: Cruiser
First owners: J. McKenzie, Elgin & Partners

Vessel Renamed	Renumbered	Year
—	—	—

Alterations: Three-quarter-length shelter
Status: Still fishing

FIDELIA PD94

Fidelia showing her Fraserburgh registration and with her three-quarter shelter. (Peter Drummond)

Fidelia showing her Irish registration. (Courtesy Peter Brady)

Year Built: 1973   **Yard No.:** 15   **Call Sign:** 2DBS
Principal dimensions in metres:
O/Length: 24.35   **R/Length:** 22.52   **Breadth:** 6.71   **Depth:** 2.83
Engine Make: Caterpillar D379TA   **HP:** 565
Deck layout: Open deck whaleback
Type of stern: Cruiser
First owners: J. Mair, Peterhead & Partners

Vessel Renamed	Renumbered	Year
Fidelia	FR120	1983
Fidelia	DA4	1998

Alterations: Gutting shelter later extended to three-quarter-length shelter. 565HP Caterpillar
Status: Decommissioned 2008

FIDELIS II FR319

Fidelis II. (Courtesy Peter Brady)

Fidelis II as *Utsiera* (INS270) with her new wheelhouse and three-quarter shelter. (Peter Drummond)

Year Built: 1978 **Yard No.:** 39 **Call Sign:** GX2M
Principal dimensions in metres:
O/Length: 24.35 **R/Length:** 22.52 **Breadth:** 6.74 **Depth:** 2.83
Engine Make: Mirrlees Blackstone ESL6MGR **HP:** 635
Deck layout: Whaleback gutting shelter
Type of stern: Cruiser
First owners: S. Buchan & Partners, Fraserburgh

Vessel Renamed	Renumbered	Year
Headway III	PD319	1988
Utsiera	INS270	1989

Alterations: Three-quarter-length shelter
New wheelhouse
Status: Decommissioned 2002

FRAM VN449

Fram as *Shannon* (LK142). (Courtesy Peter Brady)

Year Built: 1978   **Yard No.:** 41   **Call Sign:** OW2255
Principal dimensions in metres:
O/Length: 26.90   **Length BP:** 23.10   **Breadth:** 7.23   **M/Depth:** 3.78
Engine Make: Mirrlees Blackstone ESL6MK2   **HP:** 685
Deck layout: Three-quarter-length shelter
Type of stern: Transom with ramp
First owners: H. Christophersen & Partners, Faeroe Islands

Vessel Renamed	Renumbered	Year
Sunnabjørg	–	1993
Smàri	SH42	1994
Rival LK	LK142	1994
Shannon	LK142	1999

Alterations: 685HP Mirrlees Blackstone
Status: Decommissioned 2003

GUARDIAN ANGELL K535

Guardian Angell. (Courtesy of *Fishing News*)

Guardian Angell showing her Lerwick registration. (Courtesy Ian Leask)

Year Built: 1992　　**Yard No.:** 91　　**Call Sign:** MPWN9
Principal dimensions in metres:
O/Length: 26.56　　**R/Length:** 23.99　　**Breadth:** 7.52　　**Depth:** 3.68
Engine Make: Deutz SBA12816R　　**HP:** 795
Deck layout: Full shelterdeck
Type of stern: Transom
First owners: B. Bain, Kirkwall, Orkney

Vessel Renamed	**Renumbered**	**Year**
Guardian Angell	LK272	1999

Alterations: 795HP Caterpillar
Status: Still fishing

HEATHER BLOOM INS110

Heather Bloom. (Courtesy of Fishing News)

Year Built: 1992   **Yard No.:** 92   **Call Sign:** MQTM8
Principal dimensions in metres:
O/Length: 24.35   **R/Length:** 22.48   **Breadth:** 7.27   **Depth:** 3.08
Engine Make: Caterpillar D3508TA   **HP:** 795
Deck layout: Full shelterdeck
Type of stern: Transom
First owners: Heather Fishing Co. Ltd, Avoch

Vessel Renamed	Renumbered	Year
–	–	–

Alterations: –
Status: Sank in 50 knot winds and 25ft-high waves, 110 miles west of Shetland on 3 December 1994. Skipper John MacLeman lost but remainder of crew picked up safely by *Ambassador* (BCK162).

HEATHERBELLE III LH272

Heatherbelle III. (Courtesy Peter Brady)

Year Built: 1981   **Yard No.:** 56   **Call Sign:** MAEK9
Principal dimensions in metres:
O/Length: 18.25   **R/Length:** 16.88   **Breadth:** 6.30   **Depth:** 2.90
Engine Make: Kelvin TAS8   **HP:** 375
Deck layout: Whaleback Port side gutting shelter
Type of stern: Transom
First owners: W. Aitchison & Partners, Eyemouth

Vessel Renamed	Renumbered	Year
Heatherbelle III	WY170	1991
Fraioch Geal	LH382	1992
Heather Belle	N382	2008

Alterations: Lengthened 2.6m
Three-quarter-length shelter
375HP Caterpillar
Status: Still fishing

INGA NESS K44

Inga Ness.
(Courtesy John M. Addison)

Inga Ness as *Neptune* (LK171).
(Courtesy Ian Leask)

Year Built: 1991 **Yard No.:** 90 **Call Sign:** MPTS6
Principal dimensions in metres:
O/Length: 26.74 **R/Length:** 23.99 **Breadth:** 7.54 **Depth:** 3.65
Engine Make: Deutz SBA12816R **HP:** 795
Deck layout: Full shelterdeck
Type of stern: Transom
First owners: W. Sandison, Westray, Orkney & Partners

Vessel Renamed	Renumbered	Year
Neptune	LK171	1999

Alterations: 784HP Caterpillar
Status: Began taking in water and sank 30 miles NNW of Muckle Flugga 17 May 2003. All crew picked up safely by Faroese trawler *Trastur*.

JACQUELYNN STUART LH159

Jacquelynn Stuart as *Chelaris* (LK159). (Courtesy Ian Leask)

Year Built: 1971   **Yard No.:** 8   **Call Sign:** MJEN
Principal dimensions in metres:
O/Length: 16.13   **R/Length:** 15.55   **Breadth:** 5.06   **Depth:** 1.77
Engine Make: Kelvin T8   **HP:** 240
Deck layout: Open deck
Type of stern: Transom
First owners: J. Jarron, Port Seton & Partners

Vessel Renamed	Renumbered	Year
Chelaris	LK159	1987
Chelaris	GU191	1999
Chelaris	W235	2001
Chelaris	N977	2005

Alterations: 375HP Kelvin
Gutting shelter
Status: Still fishing

KAREN ANNE INS61

Karen Anne as *Advance* (INS77). (Courtesy Peter Brady)

Karen Anne as *Arcturus* (INS167). (Peter Drummond)

Year Built: 1984   **Yard No.:** 68   **Call Sign:** GDVP
Principal dimensions in metres:
O/Length: 24.56   **R/Length:** 22.45   **Breadth:** 7.27   **Depth:** 3.30
Engine Make: B & W Alpha 405-26VO   **HP:** 550
Deck layout: Three-quarter-length shelter
Type of stern: Cruiser
First owners: R. Main & Partners, Lossiemouth

Vessel Renamed	Renumbered	Year
Kiroan II	AH160	1991
Advance	INS77	1993
Arcturus	INS167	1999

Alterations: –
Status: Still fishing

KESTREL INS121

Kestrel as *Premier* (INS121). (Courtesy David Linkie)

Year Built: 1974　　**Yard No.:** 18　　**Call Sign:** 2EHB
Principal dimensions in metres:
O/Length: 24.35　　**R/Length:** 22.52　　**Breadth:** 6.71　　**Depth:** 2.83
Engine Make: Caterpillar D379TA　　**HP:** 565
Deck layout: Open deck whaleback
Type of stern: Cruiser
First owners: I. Sutherland, Hopeman & Partners

Vessel Renamed	Renumbered	Year
Solan	INS121	1978
Premier	INS121	1985

Alterations: Gutting shelter
Status: Lost with all hands in 60ft waves and winds up to 80mph, 30 miles east of Shetland, 12 December 1990.

KESTREL INS253

Kestrel. (Peter Drummond)

Kestrel as *Castlewood* (FR216). (Peter Drummond)

Year Built: 1978   **Yard No.:** 40   **Call Sign:** 2RXH
Principal dimensions in metres:
O/Length: 25.91   **R/Length:** 24.24   **Breadth:** 7.25   **Depth:** 2.98
Engine Make: Mirrlees Blackstone ESL6MGR   **HP:** 600
Deck layout: Three-quarter-length shelter
Type of stern: Cruiser
First owners: I. Sutherland, Hopeman & Partners

Vessel Renamed	Renumbered	Year
Castlewood	FR216	1992

Alterations: –
Status: Still fishing

KILORAN INS10

Kiloran. (Courtesy Peter Brady)

Kiloran as *Rosemount* (PD313). (Peter Drummond)

Year Built: 1983   **Yard No.:** 63   **Call Sign:** MBQW7
Principal dimensions in metres:
O/Length: 26.00   **R/Length:** 24.27   **Breadth:** 7.20   **Depth:** 3.00
Engine Make: Deutz SBA12M816U   **HP:** 600
Deck layout: Whaleback gutting shelter
Type of stern: Cruiser
First owners: L. Andrews, Lossiemouth & Partners

Vessel Renamed	Renumbered	Year
Rosemount	PD313	1999

Alterations: –
Status: Still fishing

MAGGIE M MBE SH170

Maggie M MBE. (Courtesy Peter Brady)

Year Built: 1988   **Yard No.:** 81   **Call Sign:** MJDL4
Principal dimensions in metres:
O/Length: 26.54   **R/Length:** 24.35   **Breadth:** 7.50   **Depth:** 4.25
Engine Make: Caterpillar D3508TA   **HP:** 705
Deck layout: Full shelterdeck
Type of stern: Transom
First owners: Mainprize Trawling Co. Ltd, Scarborough

Vessel Renamed	Renumbered	Year
–	–	–

Alterations: –
Status: Still fishing

MAIREAD KY150

Mairead. (Courtesy Peter Brady)

Mairead taking ice in Aberdeen. (Peter Drummond)

Year Built: 1980 **Yard No.:** 50 **Call Sign:** MALN2
Principal dimensions in metres:
O/Length: 23.39 **R/Length:** 21.18 **Breadth:** 6.40 **Depth:** 2.31
Engine Make: Caterpillar D379TA **HP:** 565
Deck layout: Three-quarter-length shelter
Type of stern: Transom
First owners: R. Hughes & J. Innes, Anstruther

Vessel Renamed	Renumbered	Year
–	–	–

Alterations: 538HP Caterpillar
Status: Decommissioned 2002

MARANATHA II UL33

Two views of *Maranatha II* as *Maranatha* (LK337). (Peter Drummond)

Year Built: 1988 **Yard No.:** 84 **Call Sign:** MKMG6
Principal dimensions in metres:
O/Length: 26.16 **R/Length:** 24.39 **Breadth:** 7.50 **Depth:** 4.25
Engine Make: Caterpillar D3508TA **HP:** 775
Deck layout: Full shelterdeck
Type of stern: Transom
First owners: Pitcairn Fishing Co. Ltd, Lochinver

Vessel Renamed	Renumbered	Year
Challenge	UL33	1993
Aalskere	K373	1995
Maranatha	LK337	2000

Alterations: –
Status: Began taking in water and sank north-west of Shetland, 10 May 2005. All crew picked up safely from liferaft by *Seagull* (BF74).

MARDEN D372

Marden. (Courtesy Peter Brady)

Marden seen after the fitting of her shelterdeck. (Courtesy Peter Brady)

Year Built: 1976 **Yard No.:** 29 **Call Sign:** EI4162
Principal dimensions in metres:
O/Length: 24.33 **Length BP:** 21.45 **Breadth:** 6.72 **M/Depth:** 3.75
Engine Make: Caterpillar D379TA **HP:** 565
Deck layout: Open deck whaleback
Type of stern: Cruiser
First owners: D. O'Connor, Castletownbere, S. Ireland

Vessel Renamed	Renumbered	Year
–	–	–

Alterations: Full shelterdeck
Status: Decommissioned 2006

MARIGOLD INS241

Two views of *Marigold* as *Deeside* (BCK595). (Peter Drummond)

Year Built: 1989   **Yard No.:** 86   **Call Sign:** MLQS6
Principal dimensions in metres:
O/Length: 24.49   **R/Length:** 22.50   **Breadth:** 7.20   **Depth:** 3.05
Engine Make: Cummins KT38M   **HP:** 800
Deck layout: Full shelterdeck
Type of stern: Transom
First owners: Wyvis Fishing Company Ltd, Mallaig

Vessel Renamed	Renumbered	Year
Deeside	BCK595	1996

Alterations: –
Status: Still fishing

MARY CROAN INS231

Two views of *Mary Croan* as *Amoria* (FR110). (Peter Drummond)

Year Built: 1974   **Yard No.:** 20   **Call Sign:** 2FVK
Principal dimensions in metres:
O/Length: 22.86   **R/Length:** 21.29   **Breadth:** 6.42   **Depth:** 2.29
Engine Make: Caterpillar D346TA   **HP:** 480
Deck layout: Whaleback gutting shelter
Type of stern: Cruiser
First owners: T. Sutherland, Hopeman & Partners

Vessel Renamed	Renumbered	Year
Amoria	FR110	1984

Alterations: 485HP Caterpillar
535HP Caterpillar
Status: Decommissioned 2002

MERLEWOOD A270

Merlewood as Ascania (INS259). (Peter Drummond)

Year Built: 1978 **Yard No.:** 38 **Call Sign:** 2QCQ
Principal dimensions in metres:
O/Length: 22.85 **R/Length:** 21.19 **Breadth:** 6.46 **Depth:** 2.28
Engine Make: Deutz SBF12M716U **HP:** 460
Deck layout: Whaleback gutting shelter
Type of stern: Cruiser
First owners: Don Fishing Co. Ltd, Aberdeen

Vessel Renamed	Renumbered	Year
Ascania	INS259	1989

Alterations: Three-quarter-length shelter
Status: Vessel sprang leak and sank north-east of Peterhead, 13 March 1999. All crew picked up safely.

OPPORTUNE BCK105

Opportune as *Courageous II* (INS146). (Peter Drummond)

Opportune as *Courageous* (DA18). (Courtesy David Linkie)

Year Built: 1973   **Yard No.:** 13   **Call Sign:** MMHB
Principal dimensions in metres:
O/Length: 24.36   **R/Length:** 22.53   **Breadth:** 6.71   **Depth:** 2.84
Engine Make: Caterpillar D346TA   **HP:** 480
Deck layout: Open deck whaleback
Type of stern: Cruiser
First owners: G. & J. Murray, Buckie

Vessel Renamed	Renumbered	Year
Steadfast II	KY241	1982
Courageous II	INS146	1986
Courageous	DA18	1998

Alterations: Gutting shelter later extended to three-quarter-length shelter
Stern changed to transom
500HP Kelvin
Status: Decommissioned 2008

ORKNEY REIVER K49

Orkney Reiver as new. (Courtesy Peter Brady)

Orkney Reiver after lengthening. (Courtesy Peter Brady)

Year Built: 1983 **Yard No.:** 65 **Call Sign:** MCBV2
Principal dimensions in metres:
O/Length: 24.35 **R/Length:** 21.80 **Breadth:** 7.20 **Depth:** 4.00
Engine Make: Deutz SBA12M816U **HP:** 671
Deck layout: Three-quarter-length shelter
Type of stern: Transom
First owners: T. Harcus, Westray, Orkney

Vessel Renamed	Renumbered	Year
–	–	–

Alterations: Lengthened 4.725m
Full shelterdeck
671HP Deutz
Status: Decommissioned 2002

POLONIA II B339

Polonia II as *Kemara* (PD180) (Peter Drummond)

Polonia II as *Kemara* (INS86). (Courtesy David Linkie)

Year Built: 1980 **Yard No.:** 51 **Call Sign:** MCCV4
Principal dimensions in metres:
O/Length: 18.25 **R/Length:** 16.92 **Breadth:** 6.31 **Depth:** 2.29
Engine Make: Caterpillar D3412TA **HP:** 400
Deck layout: Open deck whaleback
Type of stern: Transom
First owners: F. Zych & Partners Ardglass, N Ireland

Vessel Renamed	Renumbered	Year
Kemara	BF34	1984
Kemara	PD180	1986
Kemara	INS86	1996

Alterations: Three-quarter-length shelter
Status: Decommissioned 2003

RENOWN KY257

Renown as *Demarus* (FR173). (Courtesy David Linkie)

Renown as *Our Guardian* (PD235). (Peter Drummond)

Year Built: 1975   **Yard No.:** 27   **Call Sign:** 2JWK
Principal dimensions in metres:
O/Length: 22.86   **R/Length:** 21.30   **Breadth:** 6.40   **Depth:** 2.28
Engine Make: Caterpillar D353TS   **HP:** 450
Deck layout: Whaleback gutting shelter
Type of stern: Cruiser
First owners: A. Smith, St Monance & Partners

Vessel Renamed	Renumbered	Year
Demarus	FR173	1990
Our Guardian	PD235	1997

Alterations: 425HP Caterpillar
516HP Caterpillar
Status: Decommissioned 2002

RESEARCH TN449

Research after lengthening. (Sam Henderson)

Year Built: 1979   **Yard No.:** 43   **Call Sign:** OW2272
Principal dimensions in metres:
O/Length: 26.90   **Length BP:** 23.10   **Breadth:** 7.22   **M/Depth:** 3.78
Engine Make: Mirrlees Blackstone   **HP:** 685
Deck layout: Three-quarter-length shelter
Type of stern: Transom with ramp
First owners: B. Petersen & Partners, Faeroe Islands

Vessel Renamed	Renumbered	Year
Makarski Jadran	–	2004

Alterations: Lengthened 5.78m
Status: Ceased fishing and sold to Croatian owners 2004. Converted for use as a ferry.

RESPLENDENT PD298

A rare picture of *Resplendent* with her original name but registered as INS204. (Courtesy Ian Leask)

Resplendent as *Fair Morn* (INS204). (Courtesy David Linkie)

Resplendent as *Utility* (FR393). (Peter Drummond)

Year Built: 1979   **Yard No.:** 46   **Call Sign:** 2YUV
Principal dimensions in metres:
O/Length: 25.91   **R/Length:** 24.17   **Breadth:** 7.27   **Depth:** 3.17
Engine Make: Mirrlees Blackstone ESL6MK2   **HP:** 720
Deck layout: Whaleback gutting shelter
Type of stern: Cruiser
First owners: D. J. Forman & Partners, Peterhead

Vessel Renamed	**Renumbered**	**Year**
Resplendent	INS204	1989
Fair Morn	INS204	1989
Oriana	INS204	1997
Utility	FR393	1997

Alterations: Three-quarter-length shelter
Status: Decommissioned 2002

SEA SPRAY S89

Sea Spray (Courtesy Mrs Margaret Downey)

Sea Spray with her new wheelhouse and three-quarter shelter. (Courtesy David Linkie)

Year Built: 1977 **Yard No.:** 34 **Call Sign:** EIMG
Principal dimensions in metres:
O/Length: 25.93 **Length BP:** 23.35 **Breadth:** 7.23 **M/Depth:** 3.65
Engine Make: B & W Alpha 407-26VO **HP:** 700
Deck layout: Open deck whaleback
Type of stern: Cruiser
First owners: F. Downey, Castletownbere, S. Ireland

Vessel Renamed	Renumbered	Year
Sea Spray Junior	–	2004

Alterations: Three-quarter-length shelter
700HP Caterpillar
New wheelhouse
Status: Deregistered in 2004 following replacement by second-hand Norwegian pelagic vessel and laid up in Galway.

SHARONA LH263

Sharona as *Ocean Wave* (BCK141). (Peter Drummond)

Sharona as *Conquest R* (FR1). (Peter Drummond)

Year Built: 1980   **Yard No.:** 49   **Call Sign:** MLQL
Principal dimensions in metres:
O/Length: 23.40   **R/Length:** 21.19   **Breadth:** 6.41   **Depth:** 2.32
Engine Make: Caterpillar D379TA   **HP:** 565
Deck layout: Three-quarter-length shelter
Type of stern: Transom
First owners: D. Moodie, Eyemouth & P. Moodie, Longniddry

Vessel Renamed	Renumbered	Year
Fidelity	BCK141	1989
Ocean Wave	BCK141	1994
Conquest R	FR1	1997

Alterations: 540HP Caterpillar
Status: Decommissioned 2002

SHEMARAH II LH65

Shemarah II. (Peter Drummond)

Year Built: 1995   **Yard No.:** 97   **Call Sign:** MYRR9
Principal dimensions in metres:
O/Length: 26.30   **R/Length:** 22.46   **Breadth:** 8.50   **Depth:** 6.80
Engine Make: Cummins KTA-50-MTA   **HP:** 987
Deck layout: Full shelterdeck
Type of stern: Transom
First owners: G. Moodie & Sons Trawlers Ltd, Longniddry

Vessel Renamed	Renumbered	Year
–	–	–

Alterations: –
Status: Still fishing

SHIELWOOD A155

Shielwood as *Ross Anne* (A155). (Peter Drummond)

Year Built: 1977   **Yard No.:** 35   **Call Sign:** 2NML
Principal dimensions in metres:
O/Length: 22.86   **R/Length:** 21.31   **Breadth:** 6.42   **Depth:** 2.29
Engine Make: Deutz SBF12M716U   **HP:** 460
Deck layout: Whaleback gutting shelter
Type of stern: Cruiser
First owners: Don Fishing Co. Ltd, Aberdeen

Vessel Renamed	Renumbered	Year
Ross Anne	A155	1997

Alterations: Three-quarter-length shelter
Status: Decommissioned 2002

SPES MELIOR PD397

Spes Melior as *Attain II* (PD332). (Peter Drummond)

Spes Melior as *Attain II* with her three-quarter shelter. (Peter Drummond)

Year Built: 1979   **Yard No.:** 47   **Call Sign:** 2YZA
Principal dimensions in metres:
O/Length: 25.90   **R/Length:** 24.17   **Breadth:** 7.28   **Depth:** 3.17
Engine Make: Mirrlees Blackstone ESL6MK2   **HP:** 720
Deck layout: Whaleback gutting shelter
Type of stern: Cruiser
First owners: P. Buchan & Partners, Peterhead

Vessel Renamed	Renumbered	Year
Mari Donna	N125	1989
Ocean Reaper	PD143	1989
Attain II	PD332	1994

Alterations: Three-quarter-length shelter
820hp Mitsubishi
Status: Still fishing

ST ADRIAN KY245

St Adrian. (Courtesy Scottish Fisheries Museum, Anstruther)

Year Built: 1970   **Yard No.:** 2   **Call Sign:** MPIV
Principal dimensions in metres:
O/Length: 14.95   **R/Length:** 14.07   **Breadth:** 4.91   **Depth:** 1.95
Engine Make: Cummins NH-250-M   **HP:** 179
Deck layout: Open Deck
Type of stern: Transom
First owners: D. Tod, Anstruther

Vessel Renamed	Renumbered	Year
Ann Elizabeth	KY245	1984
Ann Elizabeth	LH92	1986
Ann Elizabeth	DE14	1987
Euphemia	KY191	1990
Euphemia	K92	2003

Alterations: Gutting shelter
179HP Cummins
Status: Still fishing

STEADFAST LH90

Steadfast as *Peter M* (PL25). (Courtesy Michael Craine)

Year Built: 1970   **Yard No.:** 4   **Call Sign:** MRHC
Principal dimensions in metres:
O/Length: 15.16   **R/Length:** 14.46   **Breadth:** 5.18   **Depth:** 2.12
Engine Make: Cummins NH-250-M   **HP:** 190
Deck layout: Open deck
Type of stern: Transom
First owners: J. Horne, Eyemouth

Vessel Renamed	Renumbered	Year
Steadfast	WK20	1983
Sustain	PL25	1984
Peter M	PL25	1987

Alterations: 194HP Cummins
Whaleback
Status: Still fishing

STEADFAST IV FR443

Steadfast IV seen from both for'ard and aft. (Peter Drummond)

Year Built: 1996   **Yard No.:** 100   **Call Sign:** MWGK6
Principal dimensions in metres:
O/Length: 25.31   **R/Length:** 22.17   **Breadth:** 8.02   **Depth:** 4.75
Engine Make: Caterpillar D3512TA   **HP:** 945
Deck layout: Full shelterdeck
Type of stern: Transom
First owners: Steadfast Fishing Co. Ltd, Fraserburgh

Vessel Renamed	Renumbered	Year
–	–	–

Alterations: –
Status: Decommissioned 2003

STRATHYRE II LH200

Strathyre II. (George Young, courtesy Andrew Murdoch)

Year Built: 1971　　**Yard No.:** 5　　**Call Sign:** MSEA
Principal dimensions in metres:
O/Length: 16.28　　**R/Length:** 15.44　　**Breadth:** 5.03　　**Depth:** 1.73
Engine Make: Kelvin T8　**HP:** 240
Deck layout: Open deck
Type of stern: Transom
First owners: A. Murdoch, Port Seton & Partners

Vessel Renamed	**Renumbered**	**Year**
–	–	–

Alterations: Gutting shelter
Status: Decommissioned 1994

SUNBEAM INS68

Two views of *Sunbeam*.
(Peter Drummond)

Year Built: 1987   **Yard No.:** 77   **Call Sign:** MGZW8
Principal dimensions in metres:
O/Length: 26.61   **R/Length:** 24.38   **Breadth:** 7.50   **Depth:** 3.63
Engine Make: Mirrlees Blackstone ESL5MK2   **HP:** 680
Deck layout: Three-quarter-length shelter
Type of stern: Cruiser
First owners: W. Smith, Lossiemouth & Partners

Vessel Renamed	Renumbered	Year
–	–	–

Alterations: –
Status: Decommissioned 2003

SUNBEAM LK335

Sunbeam. (Courtesy Ian Leask)

Sunbeam as *Discovery* (LK731). (Courtesy Ian Leask)

Sunbeam as *Discovery* (S225). (Courtesy David Linkie)

Year Built: 1981   **Yard No.:** 52   **Call Sign:** MXYP
Principal dimensions in metres:
O/Length: 23.41   **R/Length:** 21.18   **Breadth:** 7.48   **Depth:** 3.66
Engine Make: Caterpillar D379TA   **HP:** 565
Deck layout: Three-quarter-length shelter
Type of stern: Transom
First owners: J. Garriock & Partners, Shetland

Vessel Renamed	Renumbered	Year
Discovery	INS91	1986
Discovery	LK731	1989
Discovery	S225	1996

Alterations: –
Status: Began taking in water and sank 160 miles west of Scilly Islands, 9 January 2007. All crew picked up safely from life rafts by ULCC *First Commander*

SUNBEAM (2) LK335

Sunbeam. (Courtesy Ian Leask)

Sunbeam as *Auriga LK* (LK902) (Sam Henderson)

Year Built: 1986   **Yard No.:** 76   **Call Sign:** GHXW
Principal dimensions in metres:
O/Length: 26.62   **R/Length:** 24.41   **Breadth:** 7.50   **Depth:** 4.25
Engine Make: Callesen 6-427-FOTK   **HP:** 810
Deck layout: Full shelterdeck
Type of stern: Transom
First owners: J. Garriock & Partners, Shetland

Vessel Renamed	Renumbered	Year
Auriga LK	LK902	1997

Alterations: –
Status: Decommissioned 2003

SUNRISE FR359

Sunrise. (Courtesy Peter Brady)

Year Built: 1984   **Yard No.:** 67   **Call Sign:** GDXH
Principal dimensions in metres:
O/Length: 26.00   **R/Length:** 24.27   **Breadth:** 7.29   **Depth:** 3.20
Engine Make: Caterpillar D3508TA   **HP:** 650
Deck layout: Three-quarter-length shelter
Type of stern: Cruiser
First owners: J. Tait, Fraserburgh & Partners

Vessel Renamed	Renumbered	Year
–	–	–

Alterations: –
Status: Still fishing

SURMOUNT BCK98

Surmount. (Peter Drummond)

Surmount as *Evening Star* (PD295). (Peter Drummond)

Year Built: 1974 **Yard No.:** 21 **Call Sign:** 2GUD
Principal dimensions in metres:
O/Length: 24.35 **R/Length:** 22.52 **Breadth:** 6.71 **Depth:** 2.83
Engine Make: B & W Alpha 405 26VO **HP:** 500
Deck layout: Open deck whaleback
Type of stern: Cruiser
First owners: G. Slater & F. Wood, Portknockie

Vessel Renamed	Renumbered	Year
Surmount	PD295	1987
Brilliant Star	PD295	1998
Evening Star	PD295	1998
Opportunus III	PD96	2002
Daisy	PD245	2007

Alterations: Gutting shelter later extended to three-quarter-length shelter 720HP Caterpillar
Status: Still fishing

TERRA NOVA A219

Terra Nova. (Courtesy Lenny McLaughlin)

Year Built: 1971 **Yard No.:** 9 **Call Sign:** MUQK
Principal dimensions in metres:
O/Length: 16.15 **R/Length:** 15.54 **Breadth:** 5.01 **Depth:** 1.71
Engine Make: Kelvin T8 **HP:** 240
Deck layout: Open deck
Type of stern: Transom
First owners: D. Wilson, Aberdeen & Partners

Vessel Renamed	Renumbered	Year
Terra Nova	B218	1989

Alterations: Gutting shelter later removed
Status: Decommissioned 2002

VALHALLA III LH67

Valhalla III. (Courtesy David Linkie)

Valhalla III as *Fisher Rose* (LH67). (Peter Drummond)

Valhalla III as *Fisher Rose* (FR896). (Peter Drummond)

Year Built: 1982   **Yard No.:** 59   **Call Sign:** MAWV8

Principal dimensions in metres:
O/Length: 24.30   **R/Length:** 21.74   **Breadth:** 7.17   **Depth:** 3.48
Engine Make: Callesen 5-427-EOT   **HP:** 575
Deck layout: Whaleback gutting shelter
Type of stern: Cruiser
First owners: R.Veitch, Coldingham & Partners

Vessel Renamed	Renumbered	Year
Fisher Rose II	LH67	1989
Fisher Rose II	FR896	1999
Fisher Rose	FR896	1999

Alterations: –
Status: Decommissioned 2002

VESTURBUGVIN VN459

Vesturbugvin as *Harmony* (FR257). (Peter Drummond)

Vesturbugvin as *Carvela* (FR257). (Peter Drummond)

Year Built: 1978   **Yard No.:** 42   **Call Sign:** OW2259
Principal dimensions in metres:
O/Length: 26.90   **Length BP:** 23.10   **Breadth:** 7.22   **M/Depth:** 3.75
Engine Make: Mirrlees Blackstone ESL6MK2   **HP:** 685
Deck layout: Three-quarter-length shelter
Type of stern: Transom with ramp
First owners: D. Jacobsen & Partners, Faeroe Islands

Vessel Renamed	Renumbered	Year
Margretha	TN640	1991
Harmony	FR257	1993
Carvela	FR257	1999

Alterations: –
Status: Began taking in water, then capsized and sank while fishing in North Sea, 18 December 1999. All crew picked up safely.

VÓN TN381

Vón. (Courtesy Peter Brady)

Year Built: 1977   **Yard No.:** 36   **Call Sign:** OW2199
Principal dimensions in metres:
O/Length: 26.90   **Length BP:** 23.10   **Breadth:** 7.20   **M/Depth:** 3.78
Engine Make: Mirrlees Blackstone ESL6MK2   **HP:** 685
Deck layout: Three-quarter-length shelter
Type of stern: Transom with ramp
First owners: Peter Nolsoe & Partners, Faeroe Islands

Vessel Renamed	Renumbered	Year
Helga Jó	VE41	1981
Frigg	VE41	1988
Frár	VE78	1993

Alterations: 782HP Stork Werkspoor
Full shelterdeck
New wheelhouse
Status: Still fishing, but decommissioning anticipated late 2008.

VOYAGER KY336

Voyager when new. (Courtesy Peter Brady)

Voyager seen from aft as BCK182. (Courtesy David Linkie)

Year Built: 1982   **Yard No.:** 60   **Call Sign:** GCGC
Principal dimensions in metres:
O/Length: 21.28   **R/Length:** 19.91   **Breadth:** 6.56   **Depth:** 2.99
Engine Make: Kelvin TBSC8   **HP:** 495
Deck layout: Three-quarter-length shelter
Type of stern: Transom
First owners: J. McBain & Partners, Pittenweem

Vessel Renamed	Renumbered	Year
Voyager	OB336	1987
Voyager	BCK182	1991
Ocean Quest	FR375	2007

Alterations: 622HP Mitsubushi
Status: Still fishing

WANDERER III BA66

Wanderer III when new. (Courtesy Peter Brady)

Wanderer III showing her Inverness registration. She is still registered as *Wanderer III* though her bow bears the name *Wanderer*. (Sam Henderson)

Year Built: 1984   **Yard No.:** 66   **Call Sign:** MHET4
Principal dimensions in metres:
O/Length: 21.30   **R/Length:** 19.90   **Breadth:** 6.70   **Depth:** 2.87
Engine Make: Deutz SBA8M816R   **HP:** 554
Deck layout: Three-quarter-length shelter
Type of stern: Transom
First owners: D. Gibson, Prestwick & K. Gibson, Dunure

Vessel Renamed	Renumbered	Year
Wanderer III	INS161	1993

Alterations: 554HP Caterpillar
Status: Still fishing

WAVE SHEAF LK134

Wave Sheaf. (Courtesy Ian Leask)

Wave Sheaf as *Heatherbelle V* (LH272). (Courtesy of *Fishing News*)

Wave Sheaf as *Helenus* (FR121). (Peter Drummond)

Year Built: 1987   **Yard No.:** 80   **Call Sign:** MHCJ4
Principal dimensions in metres:
O/Length: 26.61   **R/Length:** 24.36   **Breadth:** 7.50   **Depth:** 4.25
Engine Make: Deutz SBA12M816K   **HP:** 826
Deck layout: Three-quarter-length shelter
Type of stern: Transom
First owners: T. Goodlad & Partners, Hamnavoe, Shetland

Vessel Renamed	Renumbered	Year
Heatherbelle V	LH272	1993
Harvest Reaper II	PD142	1994
Helenus	FR121	1996

Alterations: –
Status: Still fishing

WHITE HEATHER VI LH1

White Heather VI as built.
(Courtesy Peter Brady)

White Heather VI after lengthening and with her three-quarter shelter.
(Courtesy Ian Leask)

Year Built: 1981   **Yard No.:** 57   **Call Sign:** MALS7
Principal dimensions in metres:
O/Length: 18.25   **R/Length:** 16.88   **Breadth:** 6.30   **Depth:** 2.90
Engine Make: Kelvin TAS8   **HP:** 375
Deck layout: Whaleback Port side gutting shelter
Type of stern: Transom
First owners: J. Aitchison & Partners, Eyemouth

Vessel Renamed	Renumbered	Year
–	–	–

Alterations: Lengthened 2.6m
Three-quarter-length shelter
Status: Still fishing

XMAS ROSE FR125

Xmas Rose as *Defiance* (FR385). (Peter Drummond)

Xmas Rose when new. (Courtesy Peter Brady)

Xmas Rose as *Lapwing* (PD972). (Peter Drummond)

Year Built: 1973   **Yard No.:** 16   **Call Sign:** 2DFK
Principal dimensions in metres:
O/Length: 24.35   **R/Length:** 22.52   **Breadth:** 6.71   **Depth:** 2.83
Engine Make: Grenaa 6F24T   **HP:** 500
Deck layout: Open deck whaleback
Type of stern: Cruiser
First owners: W. Tait, Inverallochy & Partners

Vessel Renamed	Renumbered	Year
Defiance	FR125	1989
Defiance	FR385	1991
Lapwing	PD972	1998

Alterations: Gutting shelter
565HP Caterpillar
Status: Still fishing

Appendix I

Photo Miscellany

Boy Andrew (PD136) in trouble after running aground near Lerwick on 20 January 1989. She was towed off the rocks by the massively powerful purse seiner/trawler *Altaire* (LK429) but was more badly holed than had been thought and swiftly sank. She was later salvaged and underwent a prolonged repair in a temporary dry dock in Kilkeel, Northern Ireland between 1994 and 2001. She resumed fishing at the start of 2002.

Hard aground on the rocks near Lerwick. (Courtesy Ian Leask)

Being towed off the shore by *Altaire*. (Courtesy Ian Leask)

Opposite above: The crew are picked up by the lifeboat as *Boy Andrew* sinks. (Courtesy Ian Leask)

Opposite below: A transformed *Boy Andrew* as *Tea Rose* (N216). (Courtesy Lenny McLaughlin)

Alison Kay (LK57) in trouble. She is seen aground on rocks at Atlaness, near Hamnavoe, Burra Isle with *Be Ready* (LK377) in attendance. After spending two days aground, *Alison Kay* was finally towed off the rocks by the pelagic pair trawlers *Antares* (LK419) and *Zephyr* (LK394). *Antares* made the first salvage attempt but the strop attached to *Alison Kay* snapped after *Antares* had moved her a few feet. *Zephyr* then made her rescue attempt and *Alison Kay* slid safely off the rocks. (Courtesy Ian Leask)

Contrasting vessels (1). *Donvale II* (LK137) with one of the tall ships in the background. (Courtesy Ian Leask)

Contrasting vessels (2). The cruise liner *Deutschland* lying alongside Peterhead north breakwater dwarfs outward bound *Atlantis* (INS109).

So many Campbeltown-built boats were based at Peterhead for over two decades that a part of the harbour where many of them lay together was nicknamed 'Campbeltown Corner'. They were seen entering and leaving the harbour so often that getting two moving vessels in one picture has never been particularly difficult and indeed there are still enough survivors for it to be possible even now. (Peter Drummond)

Two out. *Arcturus* (INS167) leads her pair seining partner *Fear Not* (INS197) out of the harbour. (Peter Drummond)

Two in. *Budding Rose* (PD418) leads her pair seining partner *Lapwing* (PD972) into Peterhead Bay at the end of another trip. (Peter Drummond)

One in, one out. Inward-bound *Helenus* (FR121) passes outward bound *Alert* (INS55) in the bay. (Peter Drummond)

Two non-fishing vessels

The ferry *Balnahua*. (Courtesy John M. Addison)

Debra Rose. The unpowered hull of this floating restaurant was towed from Campbeltown to Clydebank where it was moved by road in sections to Clydebank shopping centre. It gives the impression of being afloat but is actually set in a concrete base. (Courtesy Sam Henderson)

A brief pictorial history of Vón (TN381)

Vón as *Helga Jó* (VE41) catching the glint. (Courtesy Tryggvi Sigurõsson)

Vón as *Frigg* (VE41) throwing up the spray. (Courtesy Tryggvi Sigurõsson)

Vón in the course of rebuilding. (Courtesy Tryggvi Sigurðsson)

Vón as rebuilt. (Courtesy Tryggvi Sigurðsson)

Catching the glint

Smàri (SH42). (Courtesy Ian Leask)

Auriga LK (LK902). (Courtesy Sam Henderson)

Seiners at sea (1): *Boy Andrew* (WK170). (Peter Drummond).

Seiners at sea (2): *Ardent II* (INS127). (Sam Henderson)

Seiners at sea (3): *Lapwing* (PD972). (Sam Henderson)

Seiners at sea (4): *Wanderer* (INS161). (Peter Drummond)

Neptune (LK171) punches into the Shetland swells. (Courtesy Ian Leask)

Appendix II

List of Vessels Built by Campbeltown Shipyard

Note: Names given in block capitals are the vessels' original names. Vessels whose names are given in bold type are non-fishing vessels.
Aalskere K373 – see *MARANATHA II* UL33
Acanthus FR138 – see *ADONIS* LK371
Active INS272 – see *Defiance* INS19
ADONIS LK371, BCK123, *Curlew* BCK123, *Acanthus* FR138
ADONIS LK172
Advance INS77 – see *KAREN ANNE* INS61
Advance II INS77 – see *BRERETON* INS97
AJAX INS82, *Argosy* INS82
AJAX INS168
ALERT FR147, *Sunlight* PD187, *Boy Andrew* PD136, *Tea Rose* K136, N216
Alert INS55 – see *ANDROMEDA* INS167
ALISON KAY LK57, *Mizpah* LK LK57
ALKAID UL257, INS256, *Pleiades* BF576, *Copious* LK985, WY170
Amoria FR110 – see *MARY CROAN* INS231
ANDROMEDA INS167, *Arcturus* INS167, *Alert* INS55
ANDROMEDA II INS177
Ann Elizabeth KY245, LH92, DE14 – see *ST ADRIAN* KY245
AQUARIAN CN42, BF281
AQUARIUS INS222, *Fertile* INS222
Arcane INS171, N907 – see *AURIGA II* LH449
Arcturus INS167 – see *ANDROMEDA* INS167
Arcturus INS167 – see *KAREN ANNE* INS61

Ardent INS109 – see *CAVALIER* INS109
ARDENT II INS127
ARGONAUT IV KY157, DA22
ARGOSY INS79, *Swiftsure* INS79, *Valkyrie* INS79
Argosy INS82 – see *AJAX* INS82
ARGYLL INS217, *Roise Catriona* T100
ARKH-ANGELL K616
ARKTOS II KY129
Ascania INS259 – see *MERLEWOOD* A270
Atlantis INS109 – see *CAVALIER* INS109
Attain II PD332 – see *SPES MELIOR* PD397
Auriga LK LK902 – see *SUNBEAM* LK335
AURIGA II LH449, INS171, *Arcane* INS171, *White Wing*s PD362, *Arcane* N907
BALNAHUA – ferry
BE READY LK377, G463, *Celtic Buccanee*r DA58
BENAIAH II B350, *Discovery* BF268
BOY ANDREW WK171, *Opportune* WK171
BOY ANDREW WK170
Boy Andrew PD136 – see *ALERT* FR147
BRERETON INS97, *Valhalla IV* LH184, *Advance II* INS77
Brilliant Star PD295 – see *SURMOUNT* BCK98
BUDDING ROSE PD418
Carvela FR257 – see *VESTURBUGVIN* VN459
Castlewood FR216 – see *KESTREL* INS253
CAVALIER INS109, *Ardent* INS109, *Atlantis* INS109
Celtic Buccaneer DA58 – see *BE READY* LK377
Challenge UL33 – see *MARANATHA II* UL33
CHALLENGER II PD212, *Fertile* PD353, *Helenus* FR421, *Ryanwood* FR421
Chelaris LK159, GU191, W235, N977 – see *JACQUELYNN STUART* LH159
Connaught LK171 – see *CONNAUGHT II* FR131
CONNAUGHT II FR131, *Connaught* LK171, *Starlight Rays* PD230
Conquest R FR1 – see *Sharona* LH263
Constant Friend III PD83 – see *ENDEAVOUR* LK173
Copious LK985, WY170 – see *ALKAID* UL257
Courageous DA18 – see *OPPORTUNE* BCK105
Courageous II INS146 – see *OPPORTUNE* BCK105
COWRIE INS67, *Supreme* INS276, *Morning Sta*r PD966
CREAR – wellboat/cargo vessel
CRIMSON ARROW CN30, *Dawn Carol* CN30, BA258, *Star of David* BA258
CRIMSON DAWN W119, N307, *Crystal Sea* N307, FR366, *Harvest Moon* FR366, *Ocean Reaper II* FR273, *Morning Star* LH444
CRYSTAL RIVER B346, BF32, *Eshcol* BCK65
Crystal Sea N307, FR366 – see *CRIMSON DAWN* W119
Curlew BCK123 – see *ADONIS* LK371
Daisy PD245 - see *SURMOUNT* BCK98
Dawn Carol CN30, BA258 – see *CRIMSON ARROW* CN30
DEBRA ROSE – floating restaurant

Deeside BCK595 – see *MARIGOLD* INS241
DEFIANCE INS19, FR29, *Robian* FR29, *Active* INS272
Defiance FR125, FR385 – see *XMAS ROSE* FR125
DEFIANT LK371
Demarus FR173 – see *RENOWN* KY257
Discovery INS91, LK731, S225 – see *SUNBEAM* LK335
Discovery BF268 – see *BENAIAH II* B350
DONVALE II LK137
DRAIOCHT NA MARA D501
Dunkeld FR261 – see *FALCON* INS117
EMMA THOMSON INS100, *Kiloran* INS100, *Oceanic* INS100, *Mamre Oaks* FR57
ENDEAVOUR LK173, *Constant Friend III* PD83
Eshcol BCK65 – see *CRYSTAL RIVER* B346
Euphemia KY191, K92 – see *ST ADRIAN* KY245
Evening Star PD295 – see *SURMOUNT* BCK98
Fair Morn INS204 – see *RESPLENDENT* PD298
FALCON INS117, FR119, *Dunkeld* FR261, *Random Harvest III* D672
FEAR NOT INS197
Fertile INS222 – see *AQUARIUS* INS222
Fertile PD353 – see *CHALLENGER II* PD212
FIDELIA PD94, FR120, DA4
FIDELIS II FR319, *Headway III* PD319, *Utsiera* INS270
Fidelity BCK141 – see *SHARONA* LH263
Fisher Rose FR896 – see *VALHALLA III* LH67
Fisher Rose II LH67, FR896 – see *VALHALLA III* LH67
FISHNISH – workboat
Fraioch Geal LH382 – see *HEATHERBELLE III* LH272
FRAM VN449, *Sunnabjørg, Smàri* SH42, *Rival LK* LK142, *Shannon* LK142
Frár VE78 – see *VÓN* TN381
Frigg VE41 – see *VÓN* TN381
FYNE LASS – workboat
GUARDIAN ANGELL K535, LK272
HALCYON – fisheries research vessel
Harmony FR257 – see *VESTURBUGVIN* VN459
Harvest Moon FR366 – see *CRIMSON DAWN* W119
Harvest Reaper II PD142 – see *WAVE SHEAF* LK134
Headway III PD319 – see *FIDELIS II* FR319
Heather Belle N382 – see *HEATHERBELLE III* LH272
HEATHER BLOOM INS110
HEATHERBELLE III LH272, WY170, *Fraioch Geal* LH382, *Heather Belle* N382
Heatherbelle V LH272 – see *WAVE SHEAF* LK134
Helenus FR421 – see *CHALLENGER II* PD212
Helenus FR121 – see *WAVE SHEAF* LK134
Helga Jó VE41 – see *VÓN* TN381
INGA NESS K44, *Neptune* LK171
JACQUELYNN STUART LH159, *Chelaris* LK159, GU191, W235, N977
KAREN ANNE INS61, *Kiroan II* AH160, *Advance* INS77, *Arcturus* INS167
Kemara BF34, PD180, INS86 – see *POLONIA II* B339

KESTREL INS121, *Solan* INS121, *Premier* INS121
KESTREL INS253, *Castlewood* FR216
Kiloran INS100 – see *EMMA THOMSON* INS100
KILORAN INS10, *Rosemount* PD313
Kiroan II AH160 – see *KAREN ANNE* INS61
Lapwing PD972 – see *XMAS ROSE* FR125
MAGGIE M MBE SH170
Makarski Jadran (ferry) – see *RESEARCH* TN449
MAIREAD KY150
Mamre Oaks FR57 – see *EMMA THOMSON* INS100
Maranatha LK337 – see *MARANATHA II* UL33
MARANATHA II UL33, *Challenge* UL33, *Aalskere* K373, *Maranatha* LK337
MARDEN D372
Margretha TN640 – see *VESTURBUGVIN* VN459
Mari Donna N125 – see *SPES MELIOR* PD397
MARIGOLD INS241, *Deeside* BCK595
MARY CROAN INS231, *Amoria* FR110
MERLEWOOD A270, *Ascania* INS259
Mizpah LK LK57 – see *ALISON KAY* LK57
Morning Star LH444 – see *CRIMSON DAWN* W119
Morning Star PD966 – see *COWRIE* INS67
Neptune LK171 – see *INGA NESS* K44
Ocean Quest FR375 – see *VOYAGER* KY336
Ocean Reaper PD143 – see *SPES MELIOR* PD397
Ocean Reaper II FR273 – see *CRIMSON DAWN* W119
Ocean Wave BCK141 – see *SHARONA* LH263
Oceanic INS100 – see *EMMA THOMSON* INS100
OPPORTUNE BCK105, *Steadfast II* KY241, *Courageous II* INS146, *Courageous* DA16
Opportune WK171 – see *BOY ANDREW* WK171
Opportunus III PD96 – see *SURMOUNT* BCK98
Oriana INS204 – see *RESPLENDENT* PD298
ORKNEY REIVER K49
Our Guardian PD235 – see *RENOWN* KY257
Peter M PL25 – see *STEADFAST* LH90
Pleiades BF576 – see *ALKAID* UL257
POLONIA II B339, *Kemara* BF34, PD180, INS86
Premier INS121 – see *KESTREL* INS121
Random Harvest III D672 – see *FALCON* INS117
RENOWN KY257, *Demarus* FR173, *Our Guardian* PD235
RESEARCH TN449, **Makarski Jadran** (ferry)
RESPLENDENT PD298, INS204, *Fair Morn* INS204, *Oriana* INS204, *Utility* FR393
Rival LK LK142 – see *FRAM* VN449
Robian FR29 – see *DEFIANCE* INS19
Roise Catriona T100 – see *ARGYLL* INS217
Rosemount PD313 – see *KILORAN* INS10
Ross Anne A155 – see *SHIELWOOD* A155
Ryanwood FR421 – see *CHALLENGER II* PD212
SEA SPRAY S89, *Sea Spray Junior*

Sea Spray Junior – see *SEA SPRAY* S89
Shannon LK142 – see *FRAM* VN449
SHARONA LH263, *Fidelity* BCK141, *Ocean Wave* BCK141, *Conquest R* FR1
SHEMARAH II LH65
SHIELWOOD A155, *Ross Anne* A155
Smàri SH42 – see *FRAM* VN449
Solan INS121 – see *KESTREL* INS121
SOLEA – wellboat/cargo vessel
SPES MELIOR PD397, *Mari Donna* N125, *Ocean Reaper* PD143, *Attain II* PD332
ST ADRIAN KY245, *Ann Elizabeth* KY245, LH92, DE14, *Euphemia* KY191, K92
Star of David BA258 – see *CRIMSON ARROW* CN30
Starlight Rays PD230 – see *CONNAUGHT II* FR131
STEADFAST LH90, WK20, *Sustain* PL25, *Peter M* PL25
Steadfast II KY241 – see *OPPORTUNE* BCK105
STEADFAST IV FR443
STRATHYRE II LH200
SUNBEAM INS68
SUNBEAM LK335, *Discovery* INS91, LK731, S225
SUNBEAM LK335, *Auriga LK* LK902
Sunlight PD187 – see *ALERT* FR147
Sunnabjørg – see *FRAM* VN449
SUNRISE FR359
Supreme INS276 – see *COWRIE* INS67
SURMOUNT BCK98, PD295, *Brilliant Star* PD295, *Evening Star* PD295, *Opportunus III* PD96, *Daisy* PD245
SURVEYOR N0I – survey vessel
Sustain PL25 – see *STEADFAST* LH90
Swiftsure INS79 – see *ARGOSY* INS79
Tea Rose K136, N216 – see *ALERT* FR147
TERRA NOVA A219, B218
THORSVOE – ferry
Utility FR393 – see *RESPLENDENT* PD298
Utsiera INS270 – see *FIDELIS II* FR319
VALHALLA III LH67, *Fisher Rose II* LH67, FR896, *Fisher Rose* FR896
Valhalla IV LH184 – see *BRERETON* INS97
Valkyrie INS79 – see *ARGOSY* INS79
VESTURBUGVIN VN459, *Margretha* TN640, *Harmony* FR257, *Carvela* FR257
VÓN TN381, *Helga Jó* VE41, *Frigg* VE41, *Frár* VE78
VOYAGER KY336, OB336, BCK182, *Ocean Quest* FR375
WANDERER III BA66, INS161
WAVE SHEAF LK134, *Heatherbelle V* LH272, *Harvest Reaper II* PD142, *Helenus* FR121
White Wings PD362 – see *AURIGA II* LH449
WHITE HEATHER VI LH1
XMAS ROSE FR125, *Defiance* FR125, FR385, *Lapwing* PD972

Visit our website and discover thousands of other History Press books. **www.thehistorypress.co.uk**